This engraving, *The Free Selector at Home*, takes a humorous view of the pioneer's daily routine, but it does give a vivid impression of the variety of jobs the settler and his family had to tackle.

Top row, from left to right: bread making, milking, washing, churning

Middle row: butchering, wood sawing, hand-feeding

Bottom row: "Obstructiveness", hauling water, ploughing.

PIONEER HOME LIFE IN AUSTRALIA

A cottage in Hobart, Van Diemen's Land

PIONEER

A panoramic view of Sydney in 1823

HOME LIFE
in Australia

R. J. UNSTEAD   W. F. HENDERSON

A. and C. Black Ltd   London

Black's Australian Social Studies

Homes in Australia
Transport in Australia
Pioneer Home Life in Australia

Further title in preparation
Law and Order in Australia

Acknowledgement is due to the following for permission to reproduce photographs in their copyright:

Australian News and Information Bureau 14a and b; Margaret Baker 86d and e; British Museum of Natural History 10a; Jeff Carter 31; Mary Evans Picture Library 13, 56b, 63b, 64a and b, 72a and b, 73b and c, 75a, 87b, 90a; John R. Freeman and Co. (Photographers) Ltd 16a; La Trobe Library 43; Mansell Collection 9; Public Library of New South Wales 6; Radio Times Hulton Picture Library 7, 8, 10b, 11, 12, 17, 19, 24b, 26, 27, 81b and c; Rex Nan Kivell Collection, National Library of Australia 1, 2, 15, 16b, 18, 20, 21, 22, 23, 24a, 25, 28, 30, 32a and b, 33, 36, 40, 41, 42, 44b, 46a and b, 50, 51, 53, 55, 56a, 71, 78b, 94; Tasmanian Museum and Art Gallery 39; University of Reading (Museum of English Rural Life) 80c

All the other photographs were taken specially for this book by W. F. Henderson, who also photographed the cover illustrations which show (a) portable laundry equipment and (c) the interior of a store, both at Jindera Museum and (b) a Kitchen at Emu Bottom Museum

The drawings on pages 35, 61, 62, 63, 67, 68, 69, 74, 76, 82, 83 and 89 are by Cedric Bush

The authors and publishers would like to thank Miss P. Reynolds and Mrs Lewis of the La Trobe Library, Melbourne, and the staff of the Reference Library of Australia House, London, for their patient assistance; the following for permission to take photographs: Kilmore Museum (77, 83b, 88b), Mr Millet, Montrose Cottage, Ballarat (34, 38b, 62a and b, 85a and b), Swan Hill Folk Museum (29, 48, 49, 60, 61, 63b and c, 68, 70, 77c, 80), Mrs Wehner, Jindera Museum (28b and c); and the following publishers and copyright holders for permission to quote extracts from their publications: Mr Eric D. Davies (*On Our Selection* by Steele Rudd); Hutchinson Publishing Group Ltd (*Australia* by R. M. Crawford); Jacaranda Press Ltd (*Warracknabeal* by Susan Priestley); Melbourne University Press (*Men of Yesterday* by M. Kiddle); Sydney University Press (*Squatter, Selector and Storekeeper* by D. B. Waterson).

ISBN 0 7136 1237 1

Filmset and printed by Hazell Watson & Viney Ltd, Aylesbury, Bucks

CONTENTS

Botany Bay

Captain Cook, who had landed in Botany Bay in 1770, had written in his journal:

"In this country it can never be doubted but what the most sorts of Grain, Fruits, Roots etc. of every kind would flourish here were they once brought hither, planted and cultivated."

Cook had also noted that immensely tall trees and a kind of wild flax flourished in New Zealand and on Norfolk Island. Both of these would be invaluable to the British Navy—the timber for ships' masts and the flax for sailcloth and ropes. It was possible that timber and flax already grew in Australia or, if they did not, that they could be made to do so. A colony in that far-off land would be able to send those valuable products back to England. Furthermore, whales, a main source of oil (used for lighting), were known to be plentiful in the South Seas.

These encouraging reports produced no action for some time but in 1783 the British government was trying to find a suitable place for a convict settlement overseas. North America, which had accepted many prisoners in the past, had just become independent and the former colonists refused to admit any more convicts. West Africa

The First Fleet in Botany Bay, January 21, 1788

The aborigines were hunters and food gatherers. The colonists observed how they climbed trees, cutting footholds with an axe, to hunt for small animals

was suggested, but the climate was considered too unhealthy; then the reports of Botany Bay were remembered.

The well-known naturalist, Sir Joseph Banks, who had sailed with Cook, gave his opinion that he did not doubt "that our oxen and sheep if carried there would thrive and increase; there was plenty of fish . . . the grass was long and luxuriant and there were some eatable vegetables, particularly a wild sort of spinach. . ."

After receiving these favourable reports, Parliament decided that a settlement should be founded "on the eastern coast of New South Wales". A fleet of eleven ships left England in May 1787 and sailed into Botany Bay eight months later.

An Ill-equipped Colony

The Governor of the new colony, Captain Arthur Phillip, could see at once that Sir Joseph Banks had made a mistake. This desolate sandy strip was no place for a settlement and Phillip moved to Port Jackson (Sydney) where he landed his settlers on the wooded shores of "the finest harbour in the world". The stores were unloaded and the fleet, apart from two small vessels, sailed away.

In this unknown land it was the Governor's duty to build houses, lay out streets, explore the countryside and grow enough food to feed the people when all the stores had been eaten. For this tremendous undertaking he had about 750 convicts, many of them old, feeble and sick, some officials, and a body of marines whose surly commander declared that they would do no work other than guard duty.

Captain Arthur Phillip, the first
Governor of New South Wales

Before leaving England, Phillip had asked for an advance party to be sent out to obtain information. This request had been brushed aside, as had also his plea for better provisions, since the government was anxious to get the convicts out of the way as quickly as possible.

Hence no one really knew what Australia was like. There had been no surveys to find out about the climate, rainfall, soil, vegetation and wild life. In the party there was not a single botanist or farmer, except Phillip himself, to advise the unwilling settlers how to grow crops and produce their own food. They had no ploughs or draught horses, no manure to enrich the sandy earth, and most of the seeds had been spoilt on the voyage out. The hand tools supplied by government contractors were the cheapest and poorest obtainable.

Not all the convicts were scoundrels and ruffians, but the majority were town-dwellers who had never been used to hard work and knew nothing about farming. Most of them would rather risk punishment than sweat all day with axe and spade. No wonder Phillip wrote home in exasperation: "If fifty farmers were sent out with their families they would do more in a year . . . than a thousand convicts."

Food Supplies

From the start the Governor was anxious about the stores. He had provisions that were supposed to be sufficient to last for two years, but when they were opened they were found to be of very poor quality and some were mouldy and almost useless.

To begin with, however, the rations were reasonable. Each man received a weekly allowance of 7 lb. of biscuits, 1 lb. of flour, 7 lb. of salt beef or 4 lb. of pork, 3 pints of dried peas and 6 oz. of butter. Women prisoners were given two-thirds of this ration.

Phillip ordered land to be cleared so that grain could be sown without delay but, as he wrote to Lord Sydney, "the great labour of clearing the ground will not permit more than eight acres to be sown this year with wheat and barley. At the same time, the immense number of ants and field mice will render our crops very uncertain."

Fishing parties were organised but, although there were good catches on some days, on others the fish were scarce so there was little saving of the precious provisions. No matter how closely they were guarded, the stores were constantly robbed; the convicts stole, the marines stole and the natives stole. The men knew that stealing would be punished by flogging or death, yet they stole because they were too hungry to care about the penalty. Within two months the first man had been hanged for theft and, later, six marines were executed "for having at various times robbed the public stores of flour, meat, spirits, tobacco and many other articles."

A sketch by Captain Hunter of the settlement in Sydney Cove as it was on August 20, 1788, shows a handful of huts and tents, with little sign of any attempts at cultivation

Government Farm, Rose Hill (Parramatta), in 1791

(Right) Exploring and hunting parties were sent out to find food and to study how the aborigines lived

Attempts to feed the Colony

As the food stocks fell, Phillip made further efforts to feed the colony. He dispatched the *Sirius* to bring food from the Cape of Good Hope; he explored the surrounding countryside and towards the end of 1788 sent a party of marines and convicts to form a new settlement some miles away at Rose Hill, Parramatta. The soil appeared to be better than around Port Jackson and by the middle of the following year forty acres had been cleared and sown with barley, maize and wheat. One or two convicts were given small patches of land to cultivate, and the first crop was harvested in November 1789. It was a start, though much of the grain had to be saved for seed and thieves nightly robbed the vegetable gardens round the settlers' huts.

Fresh meat was very scarce, for the colony's entire livestock numbered only 2 bulls, 5 cows, 1 horse, 3 mares, 3 colts, 29 sheep, 19 goats, 74 pigs, 5 rabbits, 18 turkeys, 29 geese, 35 ducks and 210 fowls.

After the long sea voyage the stock was in poor condition and the animals did not thrive on the coarse grass of the area. Some strayed and were lost; others died from eating poisonous weeds, and even the rabbits, which were to become a pest seventy years later, did not increase.

Phillip tried to find out how the aborigines managed to live in this inhospitable land but, although he had prisoners taken, they told

Saving the crew and provisions from the wreck of the
Sirius off Norfolk Island

him little that a European could understand about their way of life. However, the colony's best marksmen were sent out to shoot kangaroos which were to be brought in and handed over to the officer in charge of stores.

A woman prisoner, writing home, said that kangaroo meat resembled mutton but was much leaner. She added that the settlers picked a kind of chickweed that cooked like spinach and a vegetable creeper that was used to make "tea", though the shortage of sugar and salt made everything tasteless.

Famine

By 1790 the colony was near starvation. No supply ships had arrived from England and Phillip calculated that there was enough food to last for only four months. He sent the major of the marines to Norfolk Island with some of the worst convicts and ordered the *Supply* to call in at Lord Howe Island and bring back some turtles for food, but alas only three were caught. Then, in March, the *Sirius* was wrecked and even the weather seemed to turn against the luckless colonists, for a five-month drought set in and ruined the scanty crops.

Weekly rations had to be reduced to $2\frac{1}{2}$ lb. of flour, 2 lb. of rice and 2 lb. of pork. The sodden evil-tasting pork had been three or four years in the barrels and, when it was boiled, the meat shrank to

Sydney Cove in 1792. Notice the number of houses and
cultivated patches and compare this illustration with that
of 1788 on page 9

almost nothing; the best way to cook it was to toast it in front of a
fire and hold a piece of bread underneath it to catch the few drops
of fat.

When these pitiful rations had been eaten, usually in a couple of
days, the men stole or went hungry. Some died, but others survived
by eating grass, rats, crows and lizards; if someone shot a wild dog,
he cooked its flesh and made soup from the bones. The chief
surgeon was almost in despair; by reducing the rations still further
it might be possible, he wrote, "to drag out our miserable existence
for seven months. Should we have no arrivals in that time, the game
will be up with us, for all the grain we have been able to raise would
not support us for three weeks." He felt that little more could be
done because the people had become too weak to work, having had
"not one ounce of fresh animal food since first in the country; a
country and a place so forbidding and so hateful as only to merit
curses."

Captain Tench was more cheerful; he recorded that "If a lucky
man, who had knocked down a dinner with his gun, or caught a fish
by angling from the rocks, invited a neighbour to dine with him, the
invitation always ran, 'bring your own bread.'"

Even the officers, going to dine at the Governor's house, carried
their own bread—some said on the points of their swords—for
Captain Phillip had put his own private stock of flour into the
common store.

"The Men were Weak"

At last a ship was sighted. The flag was run up, cannons boomed a welcome and as men wrung each other's hands, the women snatched up their children and ran weeping to a hill overlooking the sea. But when the ship, the *Juliana*, came in, she brought not food but 225 women convicts and the awful news that the supply ship with stores, overseers and skilled workers had been wrecked on the way out.

The starving colonists could only hope and wait; fortunately it was not long before the Second Fleet arrived with provisions, but with far too many convicts as well. Some of the convicts had been so cruelly underfed and packed below decks that they died on being carried into the open air. The arrival of weak and diseased prisoners added to the burdens of the colony but gradually, as more supplies came in and crops became a little more abundant, the settlers began to feel that they might survive. However, life was still a struggle and Henry Hale, a convict, wrote:

"I arrived with the Third Fleet on the 16th of October 1791 . . . I was sent to Toongabbie. For nine months there I was on five ounces of flour per day. How they used to die, the men were weak—dreadfully weak—for want of food."

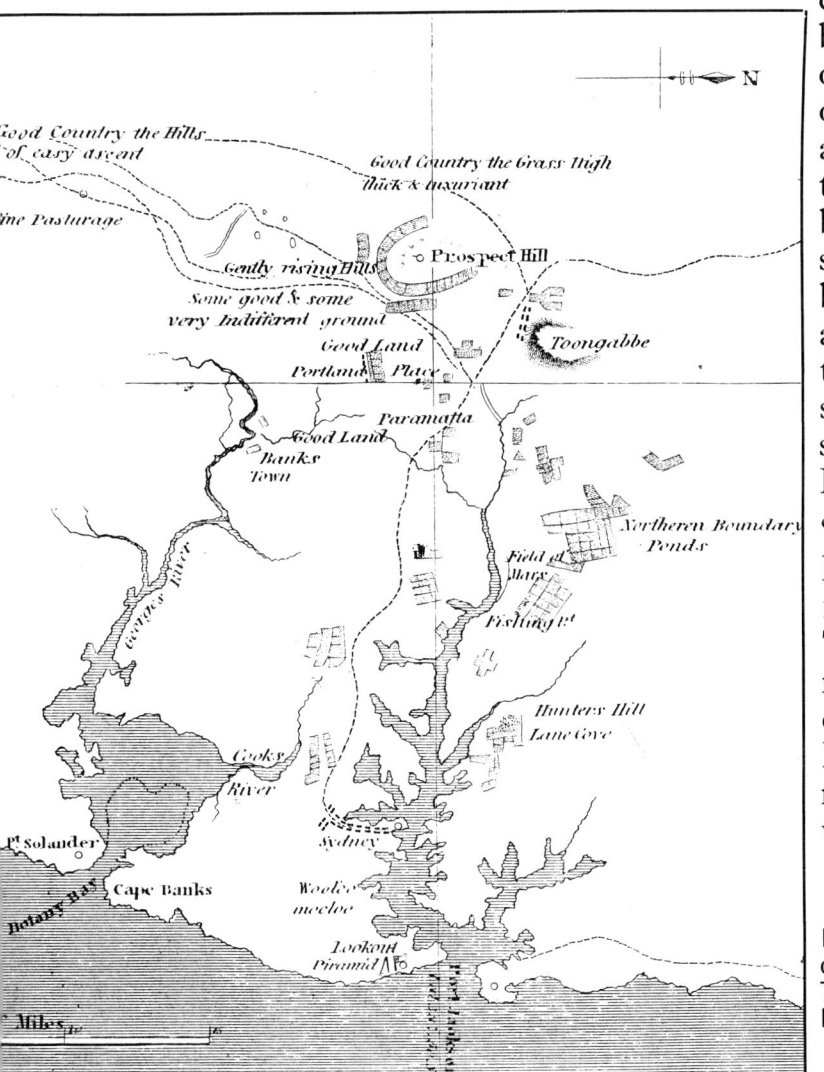

Part of an early map showing cultivated ground near Sydney, Toongabbie, Parramatta and Prospect Hill

13

The "Rum Corps"

In the following year, 1792, Captain Phillip returned to England. The discontented marines also went home and in their place came the New South Wales Corps—soon to be known as the "Rum Corps"—whose officers and men intended to enrich themselves with all possible speed.

The officers had the right to import rum and, having obtained grants of land and gangs of convicts to work for them, they used rum to pay the men to work outside normal working hours. Where a man had been allowed to make a start on his own, they would often buy up his entire crop for a jar or two of rum. By such means they seized control of the colony's trade, buying whole cargoes from newly arrived ships and selling the goods at enormous profits for themselves. But their greed had this effect: men would toil and toil in order to earn the drink they craved, so scrub was cleared, land was planted and new farms and pastures came into existence.

John Macarthur, one of the most successful of the early settlers

John Macarthur's farm at Parramatta—Elizabeth Farm

Dipping sheep

John Macarthur

One of the most energetic of these officers was John Macarthur, a grasping quarrelsome man who quickly pushed his way to the fore. Within two or three years he had secured 250 acres of land at Parramatta; his barns were full of grain and he possessed a horse, two mares, two cows and numerous goats, pigs and poultry. His wife Elizabeth wrote in a letter of 1794:

"We enjoy here one of the finest climates in the world. The necessaries of life are abundant and the fruitful soil affords many luxuries." The Macarthurs kept a man to look after a pack of greyhounds for hunting wild duck and kangaroos so that "each week the dogs kill not less than 300 lb. of meat."

But although he already lived in a style beyond the dreams of most other settlers, Macarthur was too ambitious to be satisfied. He bought sheep—a number of the poor undersized creatures which had managed to survive—and presently, with his usual enterprise, he acquired some Spanish merinos, a fine breed of sheep brought in from the Cape. By experiment and cross-breeding he improved his flocks and by 1801, when he was arrested for duelling and sent to England to be tried, he had become the largest sheep owner in Australia.

Raby, a farm belonging to Alexander Riley who, like John Macarthur, raised sheep. This prize ram and ewe from his "Electoral Saxon flocks of Raby" were exhibited before the Agricultural Society of New South Wales at Parramatta in October, 1828

In England Macarthur was so successful in persuading important people that he was the only breeder of good sheep in the colony that he was given a grant of 5 000 acres and permission to buy five merino rams from the King's private flock, in order to establish a wool industry. These animals, whose wool was the finest in the world, were eventually to make a fortune for the Macarthur family.

It was some time, however, before sheep were kept almost solely for their wool; during the early years of the struggle against hunger, the colonists needed all the meat they could raise.

Convict Rations

At first most of the convicts worked for the government, clearing land, building roads, felling trees and so on, but it was not long before most of them were *assigned* to free settlers or officers who had been given grants of land. Government work could be very harsh indeed and conditions on Norfolk Island were terrible:

"They were also fed more like hogs than men. Neither knives nor forks nor hardly any other conveniences were allowed at their tables. They tore their food with their fingers and teeth, and drank for the most part out of water-buckets. Not more than about two-thirds of them could even enter their mess-shed at a time; and the rest, whatever the weather, were required to eat as they could in an open shed beside a large privy (toilet)." (A. Maconochie, *Norfolk*

Island, 1847, quoted in *Select Documents in Australian History*, edited by C. H. M. Clark, Angus and Robertson, 1950.)

In 1803 a settlement was made in Van Diemen's Land, which was later named Tasmania; the worst and most violent of the convicts were sent there to work in chain gangs under brutal discipline and on the barest of rations. For breakfast a convict was issued with 12 oz. bread and 1 pint of skilly (thin gruel made with flour); for dinner 10 oz. bread, 10 oz. cooked meat, 10 oz. boiled potatoes and 1 pint of soup; for supper 12 oz. bread, 1 pint of skilly.

At Point Puer, a settlement for boy convicts, some of them no more than seven or eight years old, rations were more generous, for the daily allowance for each boy consisted of $1\frac{3}{4}$ lb. flour, $\frac{3}{4}$ lb. fresh meat, $\frac{1}{2}$ oz. salt and 1 lb. green vegetables.

These rations were probably issued in bulk to the cooks who made them into bread, stew, soup and so on. The monitors had a special allowance of $\frac{1}{3}$ oz. of tea and $1\frac{2}{7}$ oz. of sugar, and each boy was given soap with which to wash himself.

As the male convicts now had plates and drinking pots, with clean shirts twice a week (at which times they were shaved), conditions were beginning to improve.

Nevertheless, the savage behaviour of bands of escaped prisoners and enmity with the native Tasmanians hindered the efforts of the free settlers. The island's soil and climate were suitable for growing potatoes, fruit and all kinds of grain, yet many foodstuffs had to be imported from England and New South Wales. As one observer

Gangs of convicts working under armed guard on Norfolk Island

Convicts were assigned to work on farms like this

said, "it is degrading that this colony cannot supply a population the size of a third-rate town in England with the necessaries of meat and cheese . . . it is man's own fault if, upon an average season, he be not abundantly repaid for . . . cultivating the earth. For all sorts of grain . . . both the climate and the soil are wonderfully adapted." (J. Syme, *Nine Years in Van Diemen's Land,* 1848.)

Assigned Servants

Not long after farms had been started at Parramatta (Rose Hill), another settlement was established on the banks of the Hawkesbury River where the land was exceptionally fertile. Splendid crops of wheat, barley and maize were grown as well as vegetables and, later on, all kinds of fruit. On these farms most of the work was done by convicts who were lent or assigned to a settler who, in many cases, was an ex-convict, an *emancipist*.

An assigned convict received no wages but his master was obliged to feed him and to provide him with clothes and bedding. In New South Wales each "servant" was supposed to receive 12 lb. of wheat or flour and 7 lb. of beef or mutton, or $4\frac{1}{2}$ lb. of salt pork, a week; his clothing allowance was to be 2 jackets, 2 pairs of trousers, 3 shirts, 3 pairs of boots and a hat or cap every year, with a blanket and a mattress. If he was lucky, his master provided all these and sometimes a little tea, sugar and tobacco as extras. One assigned servant wrote home in 1819:

"We have plenty of game, both fish and fowl and no game acts to pay . . . We have plentiful fruit, peaches in abundance; lemons and oranges and quantities of vegetables.'' This seems almost too good to have been true, for vegetables, in particular, tended to be scarce for many years.

In *Ralph Rashleigh* (1845) James Tucker describes how a convict received his rations:

'' 'Come on then,' said his mistress. And after measuring the grain with a great nicety in a quart pot. 'There now, there's your peck of grain (maize) for you and here's four pounds of pork. That's your week's mess and you'll come this day week for more.'

''. . . Salt and flour they had none and Rashleigh could only swallow a few mouthfuls of his tasteless repast . . . having recovered his appetite, he found his rations insufficient; as he could not starve, he had recourse to the system he had learned at Emu Plains of grating corn to meal. In order to supply animal food, he laid all sorts of plans to trap the poultry belonging to the farm.''

On this farm the master did not supply bedding, so some of the men stole sheepskins to sleep in, while others made do at night with a covering of tree bark.

Convicts in Tasmania during a rest period

Settlements in Victoria

Governors attempted in vain to limit the settlement to a small area round Port Jackson. The country was vast and, once a way had been found across the Blue Mountains, parties of explorers and settlers began to venture inland. Meanwhile attempts were made to found new settlements along the coast.

As early as 1803 Colonel Collins arrived with convicts and free settlers at a site near the entrance to Port Phillip Bay. Here he was faced with the same problems that Phillip had met at Sydney Cove: the soil was poor, water had to be obtained by sinking perforated casks into the sand, the tools were almost useless, and seeds brought out from England did not grow. This was due to dishonest contractors or perhaps to heat and damp during the voyage; at all events, seeds brought out by the few free settlers (who may have guarded them carefully) did produce crops. But the settlement failed and Collins transferred his people to Van Diemen's Land.

A second attempt was made in 1826 when Governor Darling sent twenty soldiers and twenty convicts to establish a post at Western Port. Their first site on Port Phillip Island was abandoned for lack of water and the expedition moved to Western Port Bay, where their efforts to cultivate the soil produced such meagre results that they too abandoned the settlement.

An exploring party. Note the pack saddles and saddle bags

A wool store built by the Hentys

A few years later Edward Henty, who had come out with his family to Western Australia and thence to Van Diemen's Land, sailed across Bass Strait to Portland Bay. He had no official permission to settle but, reckoning there was little chance of being found out, he loaded a small vessel with thirteen heifers, two bullocks, a plough, pigs, poultry, bags of seeds, a fishing boat and nets. Thanks to these careful preparations, the Hentys soon established themselves. They were presently followed by John Batman, John Fawkner and more than two hundred squatters who came across from Van Diemen's Land and settled on the shores of Port Phillip. They brought their sheep with them and sent back for more, until within three years there were over 300 000 sheep in the Port Phillip region.

Foster Fyans noted in his diary of 1839:

"A schooner is now in the Bay (i.e. Portland) loading with potatoes, carrots, parsnips and turnips for Adelaide . . . corn, potatoes and vegetables exceed anything I have met with." (R. D. Boys, *First Years at Port Phillip*, Robertson and Mullens, 1959.)

After the earlier setbacks this was a remarkable triumph, but the reasons for success were clear. The land was good and needed little clearing. Seeds were fresh and the sheep, raised in Tasmania, were fine healthy animals. The settlers were not work-shy convicts but experienced farmers who knew how to cope with the conditions.

Struggle in Western Australia

Settlement in Western Australia came near to disaster. In England a company was formed to develop the Swan River district and settlers were offered land in proportion to the amount of stock and farming equipment they took with them. At 1s 6d (15 cents) an acre, with an extra 200 acres for every workman taken, the scheme appealed to well-to-do gentlemen, and in 1829 shiploads of hopeful settlers and labourers landed at Fremantle, and from there trudged twelve miles up river to found the city of Perth.

Everything went wrong. The land had not been surveyed, so no one could make a start until he knew where his own share lay; wealthy men demanded land close to the city and poorer settlers were pushed farther out. The coastal soil was poor, with little natural grazing land. The hardwood forests were difficult to clear. Around Perth wheat failed and many of the animals died from eating poisonous vegetation. Thomas Peel, the richest settler, chose a large tract of coastal land so poor that some of his workmen and tenants died of starvation. Food had to be brought in from Tasmania, Java and the Cape of Good Hope, and by 1840 a small band of settlers was struggling to wring a bare living from the soil.

A cartoonist jeers at the failure of the Swan River settlement. In fact, after a period of great difficulty the colony did prosper

FLORISHING STATE OF THE SWAN RIVER THING

A view of Fremantle published in 1832. The most prominent building is the jail on Arthur's Head (number 6). Other buildings mentioned in the numbered description are the Harbour Master's Office, a Post Office, a mill and a doctor's house. This was the port for settlers landing in Western Australia

Shortage of labour (in 1848 there were 4 622 persons living in the colony, of whom only 1 157 were workmen) caused the leading colonists to ask for convicts to be sent out, and between 1850 and 1868 some 9 500 were transported to Western Australia. Their arrival saved the colony.

The convicts were employed on public works and were not assigned to farmers, but government money came into the colony to pay for food, clothing and officials' wages. This meant that the farmers could sell their produce for cash, and, as a result, the area of farmland increased six times over; wheat and wool boomed, cattle, fruit and vegetables were in demand, and numbers of assisted immigrants came out from Britain.

Success was partly due to the better treatment of the convicts who received little of the savage punishment which had been so common in New South Wales—and no alcohol! One difficulty, even more marked than in the rest of Australia, was the shortage of women; in the 1860s men outnumbered women by two to one and, as always, it was wellnigh impossible to run a good farm without a good housewife.

A village in South Australia, 1846. One of the women is carrying a plunge churn and another is heating water for washing clothes

Overlanders

Meanwhile, after Charles Sturt had explored the overland route from Sydney to Encounter Bay, a large party of settlers came out from England to South Australia. Delays over the surveying of land almost wrecked the colony which would have starved if, as Fyans noted, provisions had not been imported to Adelaide. However, once the settlers started to farm, they found that wheat grew splendidly and the grassy plains were ideal for dairy cattle and sheep. Overlanders, including Sturt himself, came from New South Wales, driving flocks and herds for nearly a thousand miles across hills, swamps, rivers and scrubland.

A cattle station

The North

In the north it was no easy task to conquer this obstinate land. Lack of water forced the first settlement of 1824 to move from Port Essington to Melville Island. Here the aborigines were hostile and the settlers, weakened by sickness, failed to grow sufficient food to maintain themselves. The same troubles beset a second settlement at Raffles Bay and both ventures were abandoned in 1829.

This settlement was the second attempt at establishing a colony at Port Essington

Nevertheless, the pioneers had gained some useful information: forty-two different kinds of fruits, vegetables, grains and tropical plants had been tried. Indian corn or maize, pineapples and most root crops did well, but potatoes, peas, turnips and sugar cane did not flourish.

Nine years later livestock and a great quantity of provisions were carried to a new site at Port Essington where the water supply was more plentiful. Again the settlement failed; this time because ships were not using the port and the expense of its upkeep was too great.

Squatters—"half savage, half mad"

While men were struggling to establish new settlements along the edges of the country, others were pushing inland from the Sydney area. By the mid-1820s the numbers of sheep had increased so greatly that, no matter what the government said, farmers set out with their flocks to find pastures on the grassy plains of the interior. When they came to land which had not been taken up, each man marked out his *run*, established his *station* and claimed it as his own. Eventually the government had to recognise these *squatters*, as they were called, and in 1836 the Governor announced that anyone could squat on Crown lands on payment of £10 ($20) a year licence.

The squatters took their provisions with them. Bullock drays were loaded with enough sugar, salt and tea to last perhaps two years. Cooking pots, axes, tools, blankets and spare clothes were piled on to another dray, and, when all was ready, the party set out on foot and on horseback. Ahead of them moved their flocks—hundreds, sometimes thousands, of sheep, and often a herd of cattle as well.

An exploring party looking for a sheep run. The man on the left is cutting a slice off a damper to eat with the mutton chops in the frying pan. The rest of their cooking equipment consists of a kettle, a bucket and some mugs

This sketch, made in 1840, emphasises the discomforts of the
squatter's first home, with its uneven floors, unwieldy sea chests
serving as furniture, and a complete lack of anything comfortable
to sit on

When, after a long slow journey, the squatters reached their run,
the first thing to do was to cut timber and knock up a yard for the
cattle and hurdles to pen the sheep at night. Then huts had to be
put up for the master and the shepherds:

"Furniture was in keeping with the huts, a product of rough bush
carpentry—sapling frames covered with bark or bags for a bed,
boxes for tables and chairs, and some rough shelves for books . . ."
(R. M. Crawford, *Australia*, Hutchinson, 1952.)

Where, as often happened, there was no woman in the party, the
men lived roughly, "half savage, half mad . . . half dressed, half
not, unshaven, unshorn, shoes never cleaned, eating tea and
damper." (From Niel Black's journal quoted in M. Kiddle, *Men of
Yesterday*, Melbourne University Press, 1961.)

The shepherds and the men who overlanded cattle, some of them
convicts, some of them free men, were given weekly rations, but "if
the master was a skin-flint, then only meat and flour would be
provided . . . Food, grog (rum) and rough shelter were the men's
needs, although all masters tried to restrict the supply of grog."
(Kiddle.)

The interior of a stockman's hut

Kitchen equipment

Shepherds

Shepherds lived in twos or threes in huts known as *out-stations* at a distance from the homestead. In the hut each shepherd had his bed, "a hide stretched loosely over four posts driven into the ground", and the simple utensils needed to cook his weekly rations—an iron cooking pot, a frying pan, tin quart mugs, tin plates and the all-important tinder-box without which a man could not light his fire or his pipe. This is how the tinder-box worked:

"The universal fire generator was some old rag rolled up tightly to about an inch in diameter and about three inches long, which was inserted into a cylindrical brass box with a tight-fitting lid . . . The top of the rolled rag was then charred to a black cinder . . . when required for ignition, the cylinder was opened, and a flint (a bit of quartz) was held firmly over it and struck with the back of a pocket knife until a spark dropped on to the tinder, which was then quietly blown upon . . . and the pipe was thus lighted without any difficulty." (A. Joyce, *A Homestead History*, written 1843–1864, first published by Melbourne University Press, 1942.)

A drover's tucker box. An outfit like this would serve the settler on his journey to find his land and in his first kitchen

A bed made of branches and sacking

An interesting implement that was supplied to many out-stations was a steel grinding mill which was fastened to a post or beam outside the hut and protected by a sheet of bark. The master provided weekly three pecks of wheat (1 peck = 14 lb. of flour) which the hut-keeper ground in the mill, separating the bran from the flour with a sieve.

Men without Women

Men living alone or in groups without a housewife would rarely bother to feed themselves decently. Week in and week out, they lived on mutton, dampers and tea, the universal meal which everyone ate three times a day.

Dampers which took the place of bread were made like this: "Flour is mixed up merely with water, and kneaded for about a couple of minutes; the dough is then flattened out into a cake, which should never be more than about an inch and a half or two inches thick, and may be of any diameter required; the ashes of the wood . . . are then drawn off the hearth (for the fire is on the ground, not in a grate) by a shovel; and on the glowing smooth surface . . . the cake is lightly deposited . . . The red ashes are then lightly turned back over the cake with a shovel. In the course of twenty minutes or half an hour, on removing the ashes, the cake is found excellently baked; and with a light duster, or the tuft of a bullock's tail, every vestige of the ashes is switched off."

Hut-keepers and Cooks

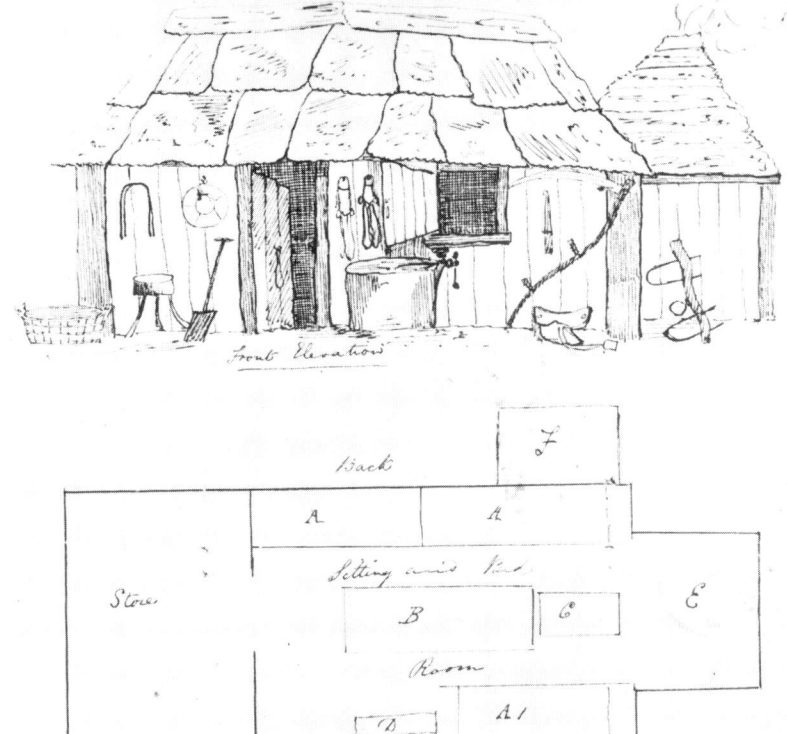

On big stations a group of men would share a large hut and their food would be cooked by a hut-keeper, one of their fellows who was too old for work or who worked as a watchman of the flocks at night. In her book *Life in the Bush* Mrs Thompson remarked that the settlers seemed "at the mercy of their hut-keepers, eating what was placed before them out of dirty tin plates . . . Sometimes the hut-keepers would cook the mutton in no way but as chops, some would only boil it, and some roast it just as they liked . . . The principal drink for the settlers is tea, which they take at every meal, and indeed all the day. In many huts, the tea-pot is always at the fire . . . We had neither milk nor butter at any station we were at, nothing but mutton, tea and damper, three times a day."

A settler sent this sketch and plan of his hut to friends at home. "The hut is composed of slabs of wood split from a tree called Iron Bark and Gum—the roof of Bark stripped in large sheets from neighbouring trees." *A* refers to bed places, *B* to the table, *C* is a sea chest, *D* a bench for the wash bowl, *E* the fireplace and *F* "a small yard containing tame Emus."

The remarkable thing about this diet is that men could work hard on food that was so monotonous and lacking in the vitamins that fruit and vegetables would have provided. There is some evidence that skin diseases like scurvy were fairly common, but sickness and malnutrition were not widespread.

However, a good hut-keeper made the world of difference to the lives of the pioneers. There was, for example, a rough and ready plenty on this station:

"Across the narrow ends of the hut were fireplaces about ten feet wide, where up to five sheep in quarters hung to roast, with one of the cooks . . . turning them continually . . . Tea was hot and black in old metal drums and sweetened with black sugar half turned to treacle. The cooked slabs of meat were simply served on tin plates set in the middle of the table . . . If the cook was so inclined, there might be dough-boys, a brownie cake or a sugar tart to follow. Knives with wooden handles, twisted wire forks, wooden spoons, tin pannikins and plates served eating; three legged iron pots, tin billies and an occasional camp oven were the only cooking utensils.'' (Susan Priestley, *Warracknabeal*, Jacaranda Press, 1967.)

At shearing time visiting teams of shearers would be given a big hut and special rations in addition to their wages. Often they brought their own cook who ''was expected to provide 'an unlimited supply of bread, roast (not boiled) mutton, and tea; but above all those natty little tasty cakes which are seen only once a year in the men's hut . . .' The shearers' huts . . . were . . . rough and comfortless. A good cook could make such a place home-like, with the floor well-swept, clean pannikins hanging on the walls, tin plates arranged in shining rows on the shelf; camp oven, frying pan and other pots and pans in good order and above all 'a bright blazing, crackling, fire.' On the embers of such a fire, he baked damper and fried chops to a nicety.'' (Kiddle.)

A drover's cook with a Johnnie cake he has just baked in a camp oven buried in the embers of his fire

Women immigrants waiting for jobs at an employment agency on their arrival in Australia

Housewives

If men could fare as well as that by themselves, things were bound to get even better when wives came to join their husbands. In Australia men outnumbered women for many years. This was partly because far more male convicts were transported than female wrong-doers, and also because the free settlers were usually bachelors or men who came out alone to chance their luck in a new country. When they had found a job, or had acquired land and sheep, then they would send home for their wives and sweethearts.

A remarkable woman named Caroline Chisholm organised a home in Sydney for destitute and newly arrived girls whom she would escort into the interior, finding them "suitable and Christian employment". She also persuaded the British Government to grant free passages to wives and families of convicts who had completed their sentences.

Cartoonists could not resist making fun of a government scheme to persuade women to emigrate. This cartoon of 1833 is headed "Emigration in Search of a Husband". The porter asks, "What are you going to Sidney for, pray ma'am," and the plump lady replies: "Vy they says as how theres lots of good husbands to be had *cheap* there whereas the brutes in England can't see no charms in a woman unless she's got plenty of money to keep 'em in idleness."

As soon as the housewife arrived, she began to put things to rights and to make life more comfortable and food more interesting. She had a natural understanding that mutton, damper and tea alone were not only dull but bad for health, especially of children, so she would add vegetables, fruit, milk and cheese to the table.

"A woman such as Mrs Candy could make variety with plants such as wild cabbage which her son thought tasted like spinach, and the yams which the aborigines found so good. The Candys were also fortunate in finding a stray goat . . . This gave them milk which they occasionally churned into butter, and once a herd had been raised they occasionally dined on roast kid, a welcome change from the everlasting mutton." (Susan Priestley, *Warracknabeal*, Jacaranda Press, 1967.)

On special occasions a positive feast would be prepared. In 1841 one family sat down to a New Year's Day dinner of "kangaroo tail soup, roast turkey, well stuffed, a boiled leg of mutton, a parrot pie, potatoes and green peas; next a plum pudding, and strawberry tart and plenty of cream." (M. Kiddle, *Men of Yesterday*, Melbourne University Press, 1961.)

A settler's sketch of his house and garden in Western Australia, 1833. At the left is the mill stream, with a mill house and water wheel. "Our Dog Jago" is sniffing round after some other dogs, and the ducks are on their way to the pond behind the trees. Other items mentioned are vines, water cresses in the stream, a pig sty and a separate kitchen at the back of the house, and flower, kitchen and potato gardens

A dough box, in which dough was put to rise overnight

A camp oven which was used for baking and general cooking.

The Camp Oven

Dampers and Johnnie cakes were all very well for men, but when a woman arrived on the scene she insisted on making bread. Yeast was obtained and the dough was placed by the fire in a tin or in a special wooden *dough box*, and after it had risen correctly it was baked in the camp oven. This was by far the most important cooking utensil in pioneer homes. Meat was roasted in it, bread, cakes and scones were baked in it. The oven's design was perfect. Made of iron, it had three legs which enabled it to stand on an uneven surface, and its lid was shaped to allow hot ashes to be piled on top to provide top heat for baking.

Here are two old recipes for making yeast:

1. "Boil a pound of flour, a quarter of a pound of brown sugar and a little salt in two gallons of water for an hour. When milk-warm, bottle it and cork it close. It will be fit for use in four and twenty hours. A pint of this yeast is sufficient for 18 lb. of bread."

2. "On a tea cupful of split or bruised peas, pour a pint of boiling water, and place the whole in a vessel on the hearth for four and twenty hours. At the end of that time, it will be in a state of fermentation, with a froth on its top, and will answer the purpose of good yeast."

As time went by, the great homesteads would have a *brick oven*, built alongside the kitchen chimney. A wood fire would be lit inside and kept going for two or three days; the ashes were raked out and the oven was used for baking large amounts of bread, cakes and pies since the bricks retained the heat for a long period.

An Outdoor Oven

In the country where homes often had fireplaces big enough to burn three- and four-foot logs, the bread oven was nevertheless built outdoors, some twenty yards from the house.

According to L. J. Blake (*Shire of the Wimmera Centenary* published by the Shire of Wimmera, 1962) this is how a man would construct an oven for his wife: first he built a sturdy platform of wood blocks or logs, a foot or eighteen inches high, and on this platform he made a flat base of wood, pug (soft clay) and bricks. Next he shaped a mound of dry earth on the base and covered it with pug strengthened with straw; he left a gap for the flue at the back and a fifteen-inch square in front.

When the coat of pug had dried, he scooped out the dried earth and fitted an iron door to his dome-shaped oven. It was now ready for his wife to light a wood fire inside and later, after she had raked out the hot ashes, to bake her bread.

She baked twice weekly and, perhaps because she complained about having to bake outdoors in summer heat and winter rain, her husband built their next oven indoors against the kitchen chimney.

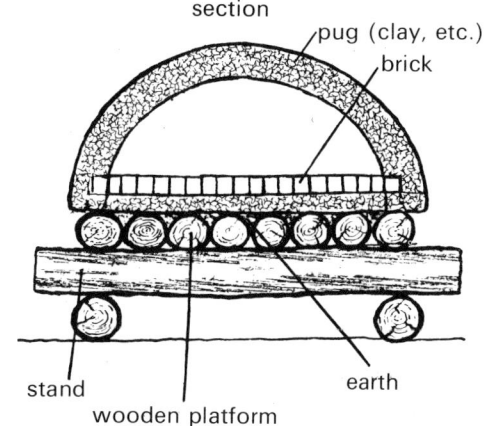

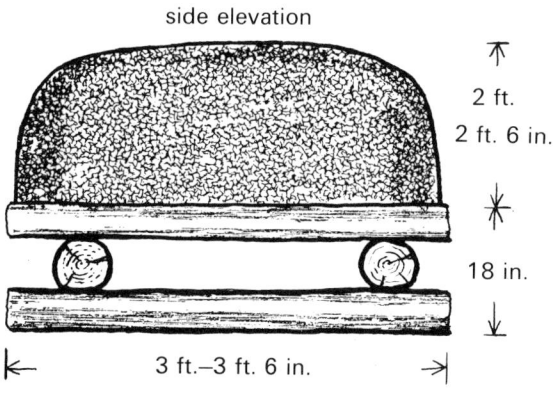

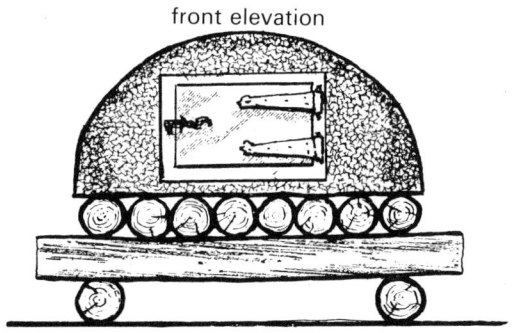

A home-made oven

The reason for building the oven outdoors is said to have been in order to avoid setting fire to the shingle roof. But in that case it would surely have been dangerous to have *any* fire indoors. It seems more likely that the oven was built outside because it took up a lot of space and often had to be rebuilt.

Success and Failure

This little family could afford to give food to others

Conditions on the stations varied greatly. We read of a squatter's home which consisted of "a dwelling-house with six rooms, a garden well stocked with fruit trees . . . a two-storied mill house with a four-horse mill." (*The Portland Guardian*, 1854.) And in 1861 an observer noted that the days of tea, mutton, damper, dirty boots and untrimmed beards had gone, now that the women were civilising the menfolk.

On the other hand, some squatters failed through bad luck or poor management. "We have worked hard and lived on salt beef and damper for six years, all to no purpose," wrote a squatter who had tried to run a cattle station at Western Port Bay.

On some stations living conditions were described as "abominable", with the workers crowded together in corrugated iron huts in which they ate and slept, and on one station, in 1860, a German and his wife, employed as shepherds, died of scurvy after being left alone at their hut for several weeks.

Others were more fortunate, for they found in Australia a plenty they had never known at home. Mrs McKay, who had come from the Scottish Highlands to Bathurst, said: "We have five children, my husband is a farm labourer, he gets twenty pounds a year; ten pounds of flour and ten pounds of meat weekly; the milk of one cow, a cottage with four rooms and a good garden, a piece of ground in which we grow wheat and millet; we have two pigs, eight cows, I don't know the number of poultry; we have milk and eggs for our own use; butter too, in plenty, for the family." (Quoted in *The Three Colonies* by Samuel Sidney, 1852.) Bathurst was, of course, no great distance from Sydney and in country that had been settled for years.

No Children Allowed

On more distant stations some owners refused to employ married men, particularly if they had children, on the grounds that the children ate rations and therefore added to the expenses of the station. This harsh rule was made in the days when all the provisions had to be brought vast distances by bullock dray and a station might be isolated by floods or drought for two or three years. A grocery order for the Southern Monaro Station in the 1840s reads as follows: "2 cwt of tea, 5 cwt of sugar, 10 lb. of coffee, 1 dozen tins of mustard, 1 dozen jars of pickles, 1 5-gallon drum of rum, all to be packed in 5 cwt of English salt."

"Luxuries", such as potatoes and salt butter, were seen only once or twice a year when the bullockies brought fresh stores from the distant town. But gradually, as the stations prospered, wives and children came to live there and one of the excitements of their lives was the visit of the travelling hawker who brought such rarities as tinned fish and flavouring essences, sweets, dress materials and flash shirts.

The hawker's stock consisted largely of fancy stuff because the storeroom of the outback station contained everything that was really essential:

"The store hut was a fascinating jumble of tins and jars, medicines, with tobacco in round three-hundred-pound cakes, besides sturdy mole-skin trousers, cabbage-tree hats, or tall yankee ones with round brims, blue shirts and blucher boots . . ." (Susan Priestley.)

The hawkers' visit brought colour and excitement to the lives of people in remote settlements

A set of nesting cooking pots

The kitchen of a large homestead would be separate from the rest of the living quarters. This one is made of mud brick, with a bark roof. Note the holes to allow the heat of cooking to escape

The Working Day

The pioneers tamed the land by incessant work: here is the daily time-table of a station in 1855:

"All hands rise at 5 a.m. when the bell rings, horses to be fed, watered and cleaned; breakfast at six; all teams to be afield at seven; dinner hour at noon; work to commence again at 1 p.m. to continue until six in the summer and five in the winter; supper at seven; horses to be fed and watered at half past eight and dining room to be cleared and locked at ten." (Quoted by Kiddle.)

The housewife worked as hard as the men. On a big station she had servants to help her but she saw to the poultry, the butter and cheese-making, dressmaking, household linen and the issue of food to the droves of *sundowners* or swagmen who regularly appeared towards evening, expecting to be fed and lodged for nothing. Another duty was to teach the children of the homestead and out-stations to read and write and, in addition, to grow vegetables and fruit to relieve the monotonous diet of meat.

In her diary of 1858 (published by Cassell, 1968) Sarah Midgley records:

"Been busy making candles today . . . Killed two snakes . . . Father commenced plucking the grapes this afternoon and Mother has been busy bottling grape wine and making tomato jam . . . Mother finished making candles tonight and there was in all 48 dozen. Father has been away a week and three days. He has bought us a chest of drawers for Mother and me, a Washing Machine, hedges shears . . . the men have been killing the pig this day . . . today we washed a fortnight's washing with the new machine."

Not Enough Food

In spite of the struggles and disappointments which Captain Phillip suffered during his governorship, he never lost faith in the future of the colony he had founded. He hoped that it would become a thriving community of small farmers and contented workers.

To some extent this dream seemed likely to come true. Where there had been miserable crops, spindly animals and a desperate shortage of fresh meat, vegetables and fruit, there were, by the 1840s, cornfields, gardens, orchards, flocks of sheep and herds of fine cattle. Even in the outback, where life was still spartan, there was, as we have seen, a steady improvement in food and comfort.

But this was only part of the picture. In places like the Hawkesbury River Valley farming flourished. However, taken as a whole, New South Wales did not produce enough food to feed its own population, and in the newly settled areas the land was mainly used to produce wool rather than foodstuffs.

A squatter could make more money from wool than from wheat and cabbages. He could rent land cheaply and put all his money into the sheep instead of into the barns, ploughs, wagons and equipment which a farmer would need. There was also a shortage of farm workers, especially as the supply of convicts came to an end, and it was almost impossible for a settler to clear virgin land, to plough, cultivate and fence his fields single-handed.

A rich harvest from a Tasmanian wheatfield (*My Harvest Home* by John Glover)

Gold-rush Scarcity

For these reasons the country was still not producing enough food when, from about 1851, it was thrown into turmoil by the discovery of gold. An almost uninhabited area was suddenly flooded with people who poured in from all over Australia and from many parts of the world.

In many a remote valley or stretch of bush there sprang up a town of 20 000 inhabitants—diggers, shopkeepers, carters, lodging-house keepers and tradesmen of every kind, all hoping to find riches and all hoping to be fed. But the farmers reported that their shepherds, stockmen, labourers and servants had taken themselves off to the gold fields, and this led to a scarcity of food and an enormous rise in prices.

Some of the newcomers saw that there was more money in supplying food than in digging for gold. Years afterwards a young Englishman named Edward Tame remembered how "we bought our goods in Melbourne and carted them out (to the diggings) and sold them for a great profit. To our astonishment we could not do much with sugar and flour, but potatoes, onions, oats and bran, sardines and many other goods were in great demand and the diggers ready to pay almost any price for them. English hams sold at 2s 6d (25 cents) per lb. . . . and American bacon would not go at

Gold rush 1851. News of the discovery of gold brought diggers to Victoria. They set out on foot in every type of vehicle

Diggers setting up their camp. Their tent is a framework of branches which will be covered with the canvas they have brought with them in their wheelbarrow, along with a very meagre collection of cooking utensils

any price, the diggers insisted on having the best. I sold apples at 2s (20 cents) a lb. and plums at 3s (30 cents) . . . the fruit was not quite ripe, but after the first load I imported fruit and onions . . . When we came to Bacchus Marsh we were offered two loads of cabbages. These we bought and returned to Creswick Creek where we sold them at 1s 6d, 2s and 2s 6d (15, 20 and 25 cents) each very quickly too, the diggers were so eager to get fresh vegetables." (Unpublished reminiscences.)

How the Diggers Lived

The diggers lived in the most primitive style in shacks and tents furnished only with string and bark beds, a box for a table and a few mugs and tin pannikins for the inevitable mutton, damper and tea. "Lodging houses" were no more than large tents whose owners charged 10s ($1) a day for the same type of bed and the same type of food. Even the bare necessities of life were scarce: water cost 1s (10 cents) a bucket and sheep farmers whose stations lay near the diggings found that their water holes were besieged by hundreds of water carts fetching water for the diggings. At one stage water was brought from the Murray River to Bendigo, a distance of over 80 miles.

Tame remembered that "the people could scarcely get bread for love or money. They stood around the bakers' shops and took the bread as it came out of the oven and if they saw a baker's cart they would make a rush for it . . . how did bakers manage to bake bread in this wild and new part of the world, with no ovens, bricks or doors or even houses? Well, first they dug out earth to form an oven, then arched it over with turf, heated it by burning wood . . . placed the dough in the oven, blocked up the mouth with turf and baked.

While his mates discuss the day's finds, a digger kneads bread for baking in the camp oven. Note the side of mutton hanging on the tent pole

"It (Australia) was called by some passengers before we landed 'the land of milk and honey', but after some four years of experience I could not call it by that name, for milk was a very scarce commodity and honey I never saw or scarcely any flowers to produce or bees to gather it . . . further on across the plains would stand a boy with milk at 6d (5 cents) a pint, but it was poor stuff . . . anyone could taste the brackish water that was mixed with it." (European bees were first introduced in 1822 but they were still scarce thirty years later.)

Bad water, bad food and the lack of green vegetables caused a good deal of illness on the diggings.

"In the open tents which served as butchers' shops the thud of cleavers sounded above the roar of flies which fastened freely on the meat. Dogs sat hopefully under the dripping carcasses. Few realised that dysentery, one of the curses of the diggers, might be connected with such unhygienic practices." (M. Kiddle.)

As with the early squatters and settlers, the arrival of a woman made the world of difference to the miner's squalid home:

"the tins are as bright as silver, there are sheets as well as blankets on the bed and perhaps the addition of a clean counterpane with a dry sack or a piece of carpet on the ground." (Mrs Charles Clacy, *A Lady's Visit to the Gold Diggings*, 1853, republished by Lansdowne, 1965.)

The Miner's Right

The scarcity and high cost of food brought hardships to the poorer immigrants and the unsuccessful diggers and, as the gold fields became an established fact, something had to be done to supply the miners with food at reasonable prices. The squatters could not do much more than slaughter some of their sheep for meat, as their leases did not permit them to grow crops. Eventually the government recognised the problem and there came into existence the *Miner's Right*.

In place of the expensive gold licence a miner was granted the right to dig for gold and to take a parcel of land and erect on it a cottage with a garden; he also had a right to graze horses, cows and goats on the *gold field commons*, which were stretches of land in the new townships specially reserved for grazing. This arrangement, which reminds us of life in a medieval village, allowed the miner—or more likely his wife and children—to produce food for the family.

Golden Point, Forest Creek. This early photograph shows
the miners' tents and shacks set among the excavations
and spoil heaps of the gold field

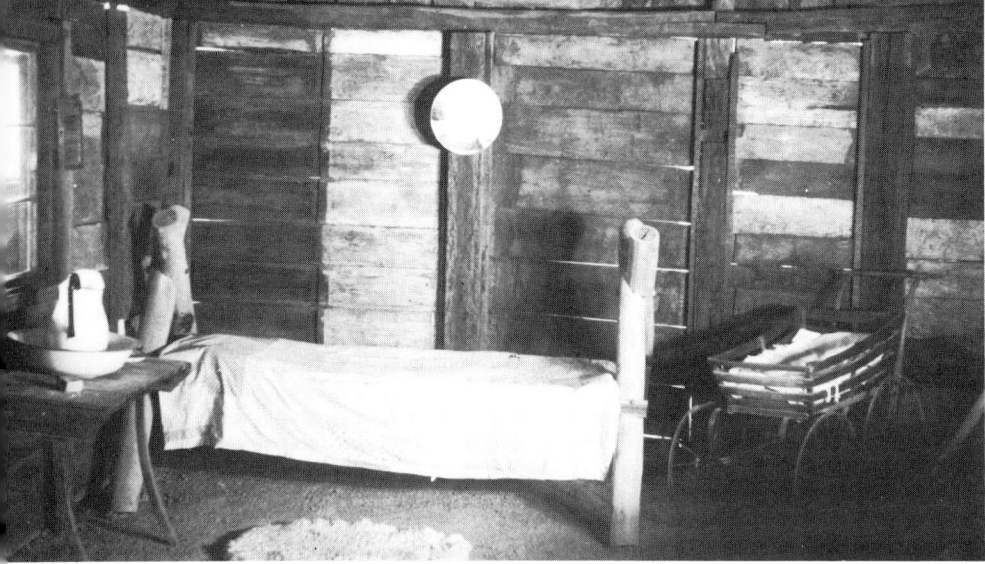

The interior of a slab hut

"Free the Land"

Since there were not enough farms to feed Australia's growing population, people began to say that settlers should be encouraged to take up farming. But in this vast country there was no land for them, either because the squatters had taken it or because it was not for sale.

John Robertson of New South Wales led a campaign to demand the freeing of land, and after 1861 it became possible for any man to *select* between 40 and 320 acres of Crown Land, including land

The selector's first job was to clear the ground he had chosen

rented to the squatters. He had to pay £1 ($2) per acre but only 5s (50 cents) to start with and to guarantee that he would live on his land for at least a year.

This seemed to be a heaven-sent opportunity for poor men to become farmers, and many of them bravely raised every penny they could in order to buy a horse, dray, tools, seeds and stores and to set off with their families to farm the land they had selected.

Water Shortage

Some of them prospered but for many a selector a long struggle lay ahead. One of the greatest problems was shortage of water. Much of the country had a low rainfall and was subject to periods of drought. Furthermore, the squatters who had first right to select land on their own runs selected parts round water holes and creeks in order to keep the selectors out.

Those who lived near a river or lake carted water in barrels on a horse-drawn sled and later in squat iron tanks mounted on wheels. These tanks, which soon rusted through, were originally used, and still are used, for bringing out china from England. Another way to carry water was by means of Chinese carrying yokes, so called because they were introduced into the gold fields by the Chinese.

A yoke

Carting water was a job that was usually given to the boys of the farm—"we had to take turns to cart water from the springs—about two miles. We had no draught horse, and even if we had one, there was neither water cask, trolly nor dray. So we humped it and talk about a drag! By the time you returned, if you hadn't drained the bucket, in spite of the big drink you'd taken before leaving the springs, more than half of it would be spilt through the vessel bumping against your leg every time you stumbled in the long grass." (Steele Rudd, *On Our Selection*, 1902, republished by Angus and Robertson, 1953.)

45

This was one way of obtaining sufficient water for horses in dry areas

On some selections wells were sunk and lined with pine and bull oak logs. Water was raised by a whim worked by hand or by a horse treading in circles, though underground water tended to be brackish and to contain all kinds of creatures:

"We did not possess an iron tank and all the water had to be drawn up in a billy or bucket out of a water hole swarming with the larvae of mosquitoes. The billy sometimes slipped out of our hands and went to the bottom and had to be fished up with a long pole with a hook of wire on the end of it." (Mrs Elms in *Land of the Lyre Bird*, Korumburra Shire, 1967.)

A way to clear water for drinking was to pour charcoal or crushed lime into a settling tank or bucket, and many of the selectors' children contracted diphtheria and similar illnesses from drinking infected water from swamps and crab-holes.

A "Newchum Mate", fresh from England, and his misfortunes with a bucket. He drops it down the shaft and tries to retrieve it with painful results for everyone concerned

In times of drought water would fetch 6d (5 cents) a bucketful and, as late as 1908, water trains were run to the Mallee and farmers would drive miles to the railway station and wait there all night with their drays.

A local paper advertised: "Scale of charges: 2d per drink. 2s per 100 galls. NO MONEY—NO WATER."

Here is a Mr Price writing about a drought: "It started in 1896 and lasted seven years. During those years we had hardly any rain, no wheat (or at least very little), no feed for the stock, and nothing but red dust everywhere. Scarcely a week passed without a terrific dust storm . . . We had a little well on our property. It was only twelve feet deep, filled from a spring in the rocks. During the drought there were at least six families carting water from that well, not only for themselves but for their teams of horses. They came as far as twelve miles with tanks on their wagons and drew up the water from the well. When it emptied, they sat down and waited for it to fill up again. Although we had no money, the well was free to all."

In some areas selectors were forced to dig wells 200 feet and more in depth; the problem of finding time and labour to raise the water all the year round was solved by the introduction (from about 1876) of the geared windmill pump. "Simplex Windmills" produced at Toowomba cost £15 to £20 ($30–$40) each and were sold by the thousand.

A windmill pump was the answer to the problem of raising water from deep wells

A settler's living room with home-made furniture

Bare Necessities

When they set out, the selectors could usually afford only the bare necessities:

"These usually consisted of a 200 lb. bag of flour, tea, sugar, salt beef, pickles, jams, as well as cutlery, soap and blankets. A few sticks of jealously guarded furniture were the woman's only reminder of the comforts she had left behind." (D. B. Waterson, *Squatter, Selector, and Storekeeper*, Sydney University Press, 1968.)

Some took no furniture at all but made do as best they could. Beds were simply poles supported by stakes driven into the ground and covered with two or three wheat bags; when the green springy poles became dry and brittle they were at least easy to replace. Chairs were fashioned in the same way, while benches might be made from logs, though the seats taken out of the wagon were much more comfortable. Gum tree logs could be hollowed out to serve as wash tubs; kerosene tins, cut lengthwise and diagonally, were put to all kinds of uses, and a useful lantern was made by sticking a candle upright inside the neck of a bottle after its bottom had been knocked off. The housewife could carpet her earth floor with wheat bags and look forward to the day when her husband would bring home a rocking chair and the most precious of all possessions, a Singer sewing machine.

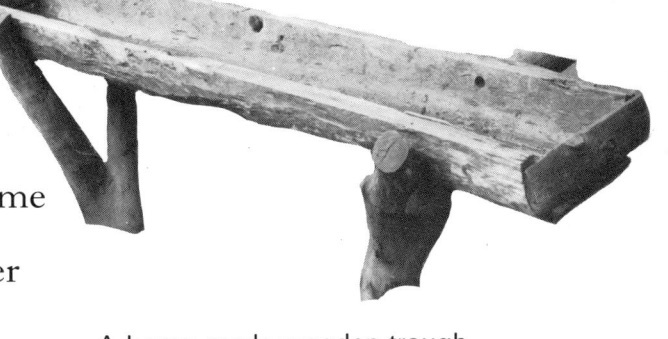

A home-made wooden trough

Johnnie Cakes

Food was terribly limited at the start. Here is Mr McHarg's grocery list for the month of November 1889: "One bag of flour (200 lb.), 70 lb. sugar, 1 case of Kerosene (2 four-gallon tins), 10 lb. of tea."

The diet of many selectors consisted largely of damper and tea without even any mutton! A rabbit, a wallaby, a tin of treacle were regarded as real treats, but there were always Johnnie cakes as a change from dampers:

Early sewing machines saved the women of the family many hours of sewing long seams and hems by hand

"We next tried to cook Johnnie cakes in the frying pan. Perhaps the reader does not know what a Johnnie cake is, it is made by mixing flour and water and baking powder together and flattening it out to about one inch thick and then when cooked it would be about two inches." (Mr G. Matheson in *Land of the Lyre Bird*, Korumburra Shire, 1967.) You can see a picture of a Johnnie cake on page 31.

Much of the cooking would be done out of doors. Note the grindstone for sharpening knives and other tools

Cheating a Selector

Some of the selectors lived in conditions of dire poverty. No doubt their lack of energy and will power to better themselves was partly due to the poor diet on which they were forced to exist. Frequently they ran into debt with the storekeeper who supplied them with food and who deducted its cost when money came in from the sale of crops or livestock. As you can see in this passage from Steele Rudd's *On Our Selection* some storekeepers got the better of the poor selector:

"Fifteen bags were got off the four acres, and the storekeeper undertook to sell it. Corn was twelve to fourteen shillings a bushel and Dad expected a big cheque.

"Every day for nearly three weeks he trudged over to the store (nearly five miles) and I went with him and every time the storekeeper would shake his head and say 'No word yet.'

"Dad couldn't understand it. At last word came. The storekeeper was busy serving a customer when we came in so he told Dad to 'hold on a bit.' Dad felt very pleased. So did I.

"The customer left. The storekeeper looked at Dad and twirled a bit of string round his first finger, then said, 'Twelve pounds your corn cleared, Mr Rudd, but of course'—going to a desk—'there's that account of yours which I have credited with the amount of the cheque. That brings it down to just three pounds now, as you will see by the account.' . . . All we got out of the corn was a bag of flour, I don't know what the storekeeper got."

A bag of corn held three bushels, so Mr Rudd's crop amounted to 45 bushels which at 10–14s ($1–$1.20) should have brought him in about £25 ($50). Clearly he was cheated by the storekeeper.

Macpherson's store in Bendigo; a store like this was the link between the settler and the outside world.

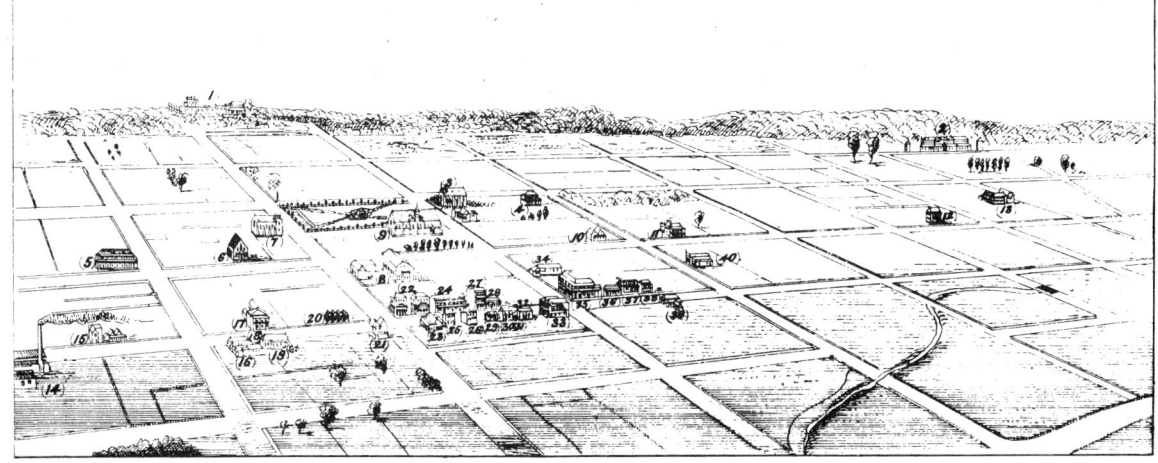

This sketch of Armidale, NSW, in 1884 has a list of all the businesses and institutions in the town. This list reflects the needs and interests of the people living in the surrounding country: a jail and court house, a town hall and railway station, four churches and a nunnery, a hospital, four hotels, three newspaper offices, two banks, a post office, two lawyers, a newsagent, a book depot, a dressmaker, a tailor and a draper, two saddlers, a shoe shop, an ironmonger and a number of stores, as well as a steam mill, a slaughter house and an iron works

Good Management

Fortunately the picture was not always gloomy. Susan Priestley (*Warracknabeal, a Wimmera Centenary*, Jacaranda Press, 1967) tells us that a selector named Goulf took a block of land in 1885, and by 1892 he had two acres of vegetables and fruit trees surrounding his house. He grew apricots, pears and cherries and kept 5 cows, 30 pigs and 300 fowls. "A proud boast with many farmers was that they never ran accounts with grocers or ironmongers but sold butter, cheese and eggs to keep them square. Some of the German families . . . grew the whole range of fruit and vegetables, killed their own meat, made sausages and other small goods, ground their own wheatmeal for bread and oats for their porridge, dried grapes for currant tarts and pressed their own wine."

Household management like this was only possible when a woman took charge: Mrs Elms recalled in *Land of the Lyre Bird*: "Before I arrived, my brother had not troubled to milk a cow, and of course when he first started to clear the scrub there was no grass to feed one, so his fare was salt meat, bread, rice, treacle and tea without milk, so it seemed quite a luxury to have plenty of milk, cream and butter. My first butter was churned in the milk bucket with a large home-made wooden spoon. Later on we built a small dairy and used to put the butter into casks to send away, for at that time butter factories and separators were not even thought of."

A Travelling Hawker

Like squatters the lonely selectors welcomed the coming of a travelling hawker who was usually a Hindu or a Muslim from India. Every year some twelve hundred Asians made their way to Melbourne to renew their licences. Nagassa Singh was one of these hawkers; he carried "the usual bundle which contained men's shirts and working clothes, handkerchiefs, Indian silks, cottons, buttons, and scissors . . . The bundle of goods was tied on his back with, over one shoulder, yards of unbleached calico. On top of the bundle was a small trunk. In one hand, wrapped in a tea-towel, he carried a fry-pan, a small saucepan, a tin of curry powder, and a knife, fork and spoon. In the other hand was a blackened billy, containing an enamelled mug, sugar and tea.

"With this load Nagassa Singh set out to walk from Melbourne to the West . . . He was a practical salesman. When the bundle was unrolled, the first articles to appear were the most necessary—working clothes, then to catch the eye of the women came the gaily coloured silks; finally when sales seemed exhausted, he would produce the small items—buttons, scissors, tinned fish and sweets. Finally he would end the sale by demanding a tin dish and some sugar. Then dexterously he would spin the sugar to make for the children Turkish lolly (we know it as Fairy Floss). Nagassa Singh always insisted that each child have some of his curry. No wonder the children loved the hawker's visit.

"Nagassa Singh prospered sufficiently to obtain a horse and dog cart . . . Then finally he obtained the hawker's dream—a wagon

A butcher's delivery cart

Two drapers' vehicles: one, an Indian hawker's horse-drawn cart, and the other an early truck

A butcher's shop in Wagga Wagga, 1874

built above the wheels so that both sides and the back could be let down to serve as display counters. In such a wagon he carried almost as much as the contents of a small country store." (L. J. Blake, *Shire of the Wimmera Centenary*, Shire of the Wimmera, 1962.)

A Local Butcher

Where a number of farms lay reasonably close together, a butcher and a baker might come round with fresh meat and loaves. At Mildura in 1888 the local butcher was Tom Barton; he "lived in a lined tent near a tree where he hung a beast or a sheep which he had killed. He would carry it around, a side at a time on his shoulder until he bought a horse. He then carried two at once, one side hanging from each side of the horse. He cut joints alternately to keep the balance." (A. Lapthorne, *Mildura Calling*, Mildura Gallery Society, 1965.)

53

Vegetables

From the squatters' homesteads and the selectors' little farmhouses, let us turn to the towns to see how people were faring in their everyday lives during the middle years of the 19th century.

Food was no longer scarce, for in normal times there were ample supplies of home-grown wheat and meat. Vegetable growing, however, seemed to make no appeal to the Australians. To the "currency lads" (freeborn Australians) it was work that had formerly been carried out by convicts, and in any case hot sunshine, periods of drought and a shortage of good seeds made gardening a difficult art.

At all events little commercial vegetable growing took place until the arrival of the Chinese. During the 1840s, when the supply of convicts was dwindling, numbers of Chinese were brought to Australia as cheap labour. Then, with the discovery of gold, they flocked into the country and in three years 40 000 Chinese had arrived on the Victorian gold fields. Most of them came in the hope of finding gold but, as the white men became hostile, and laws were passed to exclude them from the gold fields, many were glad to return home.

A Chinese market gardener

A Chinese market garden on the banks of a creek in Melbourne

The Chinese were also excellent cooks. Some worked on stations and the successful few ran restaurants like this one at Ballarat

Some of those who stayed turned to vegetable growing. Patient, industrious and accustomed to making a living from a small patch of earth, they succeeded where most men would have failed. On smallholdings in the valleys of creeks they raised vegetables in the alluvial soil and watered them with creek-water fetched in cans suspended from a yoke. Then they would go from house to house with baskets of produce for sale. Three generations of housewives relied on Johnnie Chinaman to bring them fresh vegetables in season and there was hardly a patch of land along the creeks which surround Melbourne that was not a Chinese market garden.

As transport improved and vegetable growing became a mechanised industry, the smallholders went out of business, but to this day much of the fruit and vegetable marketing is in Chinese hands.

Settlers outside their hut in the bush

This sketch of an Australian kitchen in the 1880s shows the cook roasting a joint, hanging from a jack. Often a batter pudding was placed on the grate underneath so that it caught the juices from the meat and cooked in the heat from the fire

Makeshift Homes

In the 1850s newcomers to Australia were fascinated and often taken aback by the conditions of life in this remote southern country. Some were surprised to find that most of the working people earned more and ate better than in England; others were shocked by the squalor of Sydney and the ramshackle homes that they saw on every side.

The wooden cradle on the left is a replica of an English one, designed to keep the baby safe from cold draughts. The settler's wife soon found that an airy wickerwork basket was more suitable for Australian conditions

F. Lancelot, writing about farmers in *Australia as It Is*, 1852, noted that "their domestic furniture and appliances are all of the coarse makeshift kind; this is not occasioned by poverty, for most of them could, if they choose, live in splendid houses . . . it simply proceeds from their desire to purchase a score of fruit trees, a cow or a pig in preference to a stuffed chair, sofa or polished table."

A Select Committee of 1860 reported to the Legislative Assembly of New South Wales that working men's homes had none of the "superior contrivances" such as indoor sinks, cooking stoves and fitted pantries which were "so great a comfort to the humble housewife in England."

More than twenty years later R. E. N. Twopenny found food cheaper and more plentiful than in England, but he noticed that:

"The kitchen is ordinarily very poorly provided with utensils. Ranges and stoves are usually found only in the wealthier homes—the usual cooking apparatus being a colonial oven—a sort of box with a fire above and below, which is very convenient for burning wood, the usual fuel throughout Australia." (*Town Life in Australia*, 1883.)

The fact of the matter was that in a country whose fringes had been settled for less than a hundred years, whose interior was still not fully explored, the people were still battling to establish themselves. Most manufactured goods, from kitchen utensils to baths and corrugated iron sheets, had to be brought from the other side of the world and then transported over huge distances by bullock dray, so people went without "luxuries" and made the best of what they had.

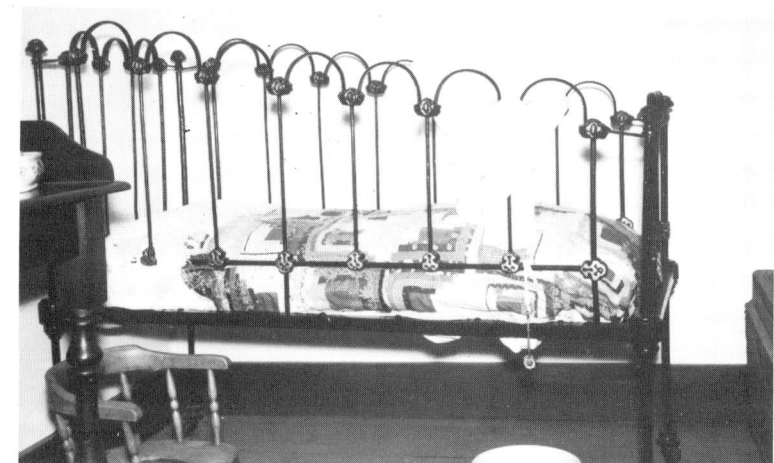

(Top left) Sitting room furniture, elaborately carved and turned, (top right) a chandelier with pendent crystal lustres and (right) a child's cast-iron bed, all needing constant dusting and polishing

Lack of Servants

In large mansions whose owners could afford to import the latest furnishings, life was elegant and comfortable, though there was a good deal of grumbling about the shortage of cooks and maid-servants. A small army of servants was needed to carry out all the sweeping, dusting and polishing, the black-leading of grates, the preparation of meals, the carrying of hot water upstairs and the washing of clothes. In England, with a large population and a good deal of unemployment, servants were cheap and plentiful but in Australia they were scarce, expensive and difficult to keep.

"Of course there are some good servants," remarked R. E. N. Twopenny, "but unfortunately for their employers the butchers and bakers generally have a keen eye for such, arguing with great justice that a good servant is likely to make a good wife."

The Weekly Wash

Lack of servants, a hot climate and frequent droughts compelled the Australians to find ways to overcome their problems. Hence we find, for example, that Australian housewives were using washing machines and methods of refrigeration long before their English sisters.

All the women and girls of the homestead would be enlisted to help with the weekly wash. In the bush they would boil the clothes in a cast-iron *try-pot* or in a kerosene tin over an open fire near the water supply. Kerosene tins were much used as miniature coppers and were also cut in halves diagonally to make water troughs. An essential item for laundry work was the wash-board on which clothes were vigorously rubbed up and down to squeeze out the dirt.

The simplest laundry equipment was a try-pot for heating water, wooden buckets, wooden dollies for pounding the dirty clothes, troughs made from kerosene tins, washboards and flat irons

Wash-day Excursion

An improvement on the try-pot and kerosene tin was the cast-iron copper. On wash days the copper would be carried into the open and filled with water; a fire was lit in the fire-box underneath in order to boil the clothes which were stirred, prodded and lifted out with a copper stick. In times of drought clothes, copper and rinsing tubs would be loaded on a dray and taken to the nearest dam, river or water hole. The mother of one of the authors of this book remembers these delightful excursions to a dam some miles away which had supplied the old gold fields; she and her sisters would feed the fire and play while their mother did the washing.

Other children used the spare wash tubs as boats and paddled themselves about on the water.

On big stations the copper would be sited in a special laundry hut, and in town mansions, and later in small middle-class homes, bricked-in coppers were installed in a wash-house in the yard.

This advertisement for a "washing machine" shows how the laundry was often done at some distance from the house and near a water supply

Washing Machines

In the 1850s there appeared on the market a new device called a *washing machine*. Sarah Midgley's father brought one home in 1858 and she wrote in her diary, "... today we washed a fortnight's washing with the new machine ..." Sarah does not describe the machine in detail, but we can be sure that it worked by moving the clothes about in hot soapy water in order to loosen the dirt. This had previously been done by pounding the clothes on a rock or rubbing them on a wash-board or working them about in a tub with a *washing dolly*.

Various types of washing machine came on the market, each apparently more efficient than anything so far invented. Here is *Hutton's Patent Australian Washing Machine* about which *Frearson's Weekly* of June 20, 1878, reported:

"This machine accomplishes the work of washing clothes or anything of like nature by a combination of four things, viz., hot air, dash of water, rubbing over fluted surfaces and by continual presentation of fresh surfaces to be operated on."

The manufacturer claimed that it was especially suitable for farmers because of the small amount of water it required, yet a child of ten could wash thirty shirts in it in five minutes!

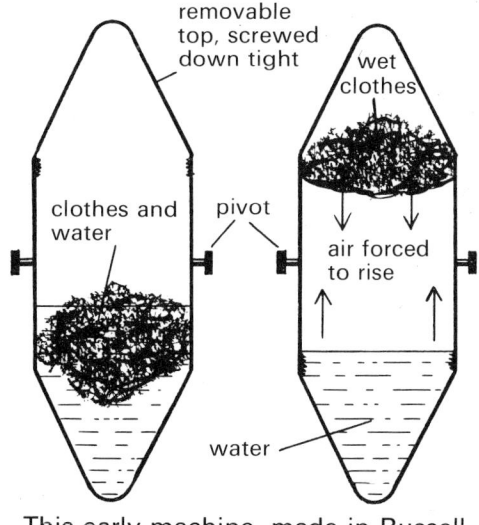

This early machine, made in Russell Street, Melbourne, in 1854, worked on the vacuum principle. When the "torpedo" was turned upside down, the clothes were pressed down on trapped air; the air forced its way through and so put pressure on the dirt

Hutton's Patent Australian Washing Machine of 1878

This 1890 machine combines the action of two traditional washing aids. The tub has a corrugated lining like a washboard and the agitator is shaped like a washing dolly

The fact that a machine could be worked by a child seems to have been a good selling point, for *Lowe's Patent Washing Machine* of 1890, a most advanced model in galvanised iron with a fire stand for £5 ($10), or in copper for £8.15s ($17.50), was "especially convenient in the homes where the wife does her own housework, for the children can work it." This sounds, in fact, as if she shared the housework with the children! However, no matter who worked it, Lowe's machine would do a fortnight's washing for a family of eight or ten in two or three hours.

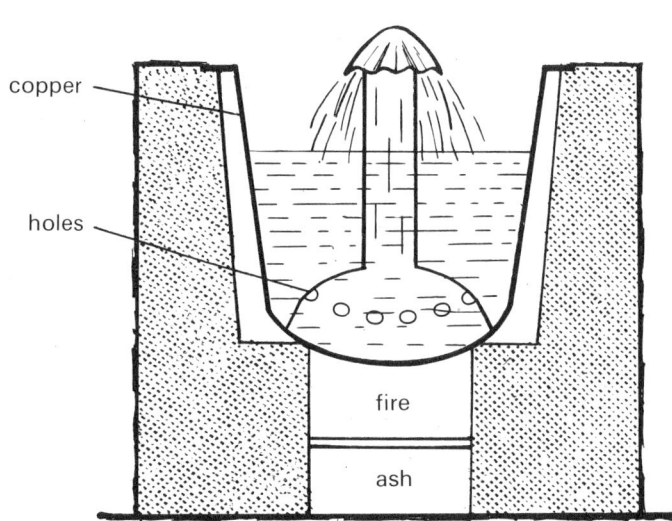

copper

holes

fire

ash

This washing funnel was placed in the copper and the water gushed up the funnel and cascaded over the clothes

The Antipodean Cooking Book of 1895 told the housewife who could not afford to buy a washing machine how to make a model. She should place in her copper a large funnel which would cause the boiling water to gush up the inverted funnel and cascade over the clothes. This simple process seems to have been quite popular in some districts and may have led to the use of a funnel in commercial machines. In the *Zwar Patent Vacuum Model Washing Machine* (rather expensive at £15 ($30)) an inverted funnel was pumped up and down by a lever, though in this case the funnel merely worked like a hand grabbing the clothes and pummelling them up and down.

Many washing machines were shaped like barrels. A handle at the side worked paddles which agitated the clothes inside the washer. This is the Lilywhite Washing Machine, a very popular model at the turn of the century

Manufacturers stressed in their advertising that their machines were so easy to use that a child could work them

The Osmond Little Marvel Washing Machine also used funnels, but in this case the housewife had to move the gadget up and down in her wash tub or copper

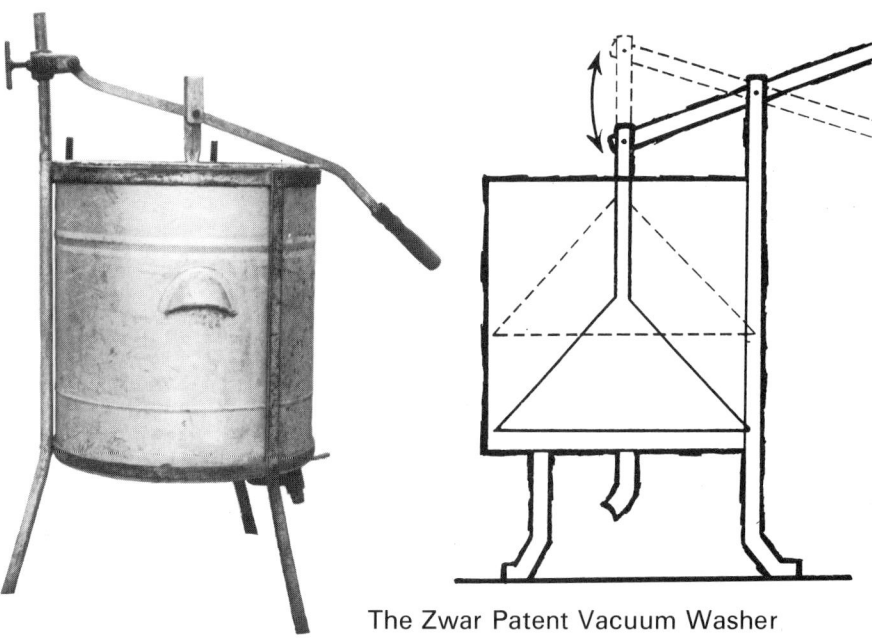

The Zwar Patent Vacuum Washer

Mangles

Having washed the clothes, the housewife had to dry and iron them, and this she began to do at the side of the river or dam, wringing the clothes by hand and spreading them on bushes. When wash day took place at home, she usually passed them through the *mangle*, a formidable machine with cast-iron legs and sides and two wooden rollers which were made to revolve by turning a handle. When the clothes were fed into the rollers, the water squeezed out of them dripped into a tub placed underneath. Sheets, pillowslips, blankets and such plain articles went through easily, but you had to be careful with shirts and dresses in case the buttons got broken.

A very large box mangle from a Victorian mansion where great quantities of household linen would need to be handled every washday

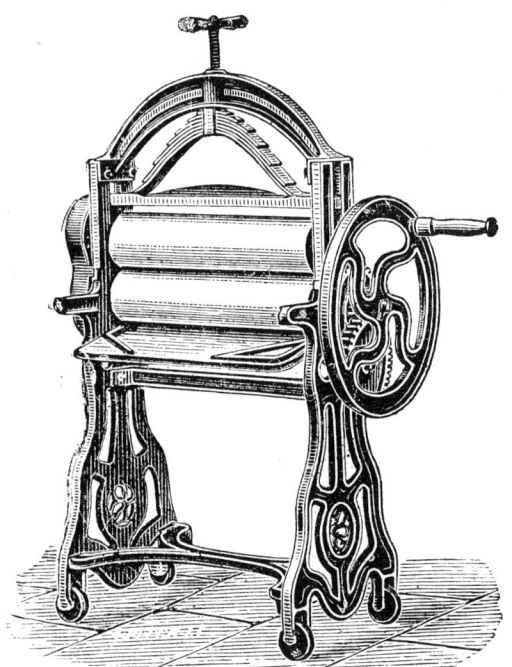

Mangles

Mangling was hard work and small boys, intent upon improving their muscles, were encouraged to help their mother, though she had to keep a sharp eye on them since crushed fingers were an all too common penalty for over-enthusiasm! "Taking in mangling" was one of the ways in which a poor woman could earn some extra money; she would do this work and perhaps the ironing too for a well-to-do household. Mangling not only squeezed the clothes almost dry but it reduced the need to iron big articles like sheets which were folded and passed through the mangle and given a final smoothing with the iron.

Wringers

Mangles were very widely used and, being more or less indestructible, they are still to be seen in junkyards and dumps. Eventually they gave way to the smaller and neater wringer, though in 1885 Pierce and Co. of Melbourne were offering for sale an ingenious contraption consisting of a washing machine with a mangle mounted on top; its advantage was presumably that it took up less space than two separate machines. The wringer on its stand or screwed to the side of a trough was to be found in every home laundry up to, and even after, World War II. Many electric washing machines included a built-in wringer of similar type, but nowadays spin-dryers are more usual.

This wringer, its stand and its tubs were designed so that they could easily be transported to the nearest source of water

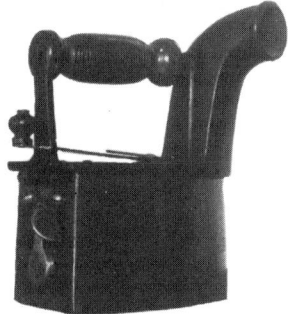

Tailor's iron

Irons

Washed, wrung out or mangled, the clothes had finally to be ironed, and for many years every home had several *flat irons* which were heated on the stove or in the fire itself. The housewife protected her hands by using an iron-holder, one of the first things a little girl would learn to make in her sewing lessons. The sole of the iron always had to be wiped clean on a rag, but there was less risk of smuts ruining the clean wash if the housewife owned a *box iron* in which hot coals were placed. It could be bought with a right-hand or left-hand chimney and, when it began to cool, the housewife would swing the iron to and fro or step outside into the wind to make the coals burn more brightly.

Box iron

Gas irons, normally only available in towns, were much superior to the various types of flat iron because they could be kept at a steady heat; a flexible pipe brought the gas to a number of small jets which were lit like a gas stove. Another successor to the flat iron, and a boon to housewives on remote farms, was the *petrol-pressure iron* which worked on the same principle as the gas iron, the fuel in this case being petrol which was supplied to an adjustable jet from a small container attached to the iron itself.

Billet iron—a block of iron was heated and slipped inside the iron

An early gas iron

Two flat-iron stands, one for a small household and one for a mansion or institution

Petrol iron

Spirit iron—it was heated by burning rags, soaked in methylated spirits, inside the iron

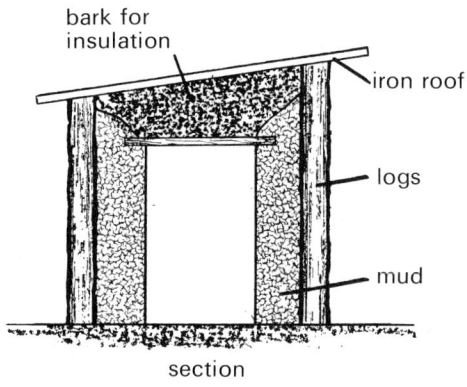

bark for insulation

iron roof

logs

mud

section

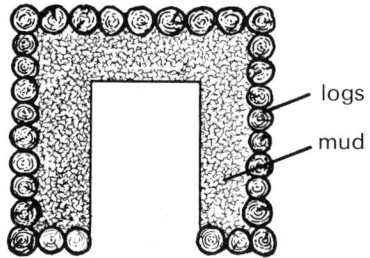

logs

mud

The walls of this mud-brick cool room are two feet thick

Section and plan of a cool room showing the thickness of insulation required to maintain a cool temperature inside

Hot Weather

Anyone who has experienced the heat of an Australian summer must have wondered how, in days long before fridges were invented, the pioneers managed to keep food in an edible condition. In the early days they simply did the best that they could; meat had to be eaten on the very day it was killed; butter was kept in a bucket down the well and in towns the milkman came round twice a day because the morning's milk would be sour by evening.

A Cool Room

Once homes had been built and as soon as wives arrived, the problem was tackled in various ways. One of the first things to do was to build a *cool room*, a small store with mud-brick walls so thick—two feet and more—that they would keep the heat out. The roof was insulated with layers of stringy bark and the whole place was made as fly-proof as possible by nailing muslin or fine wire mesh over the window. Sometimes the mud walls were given an outer skin of logs which were placed upright all round the store room.

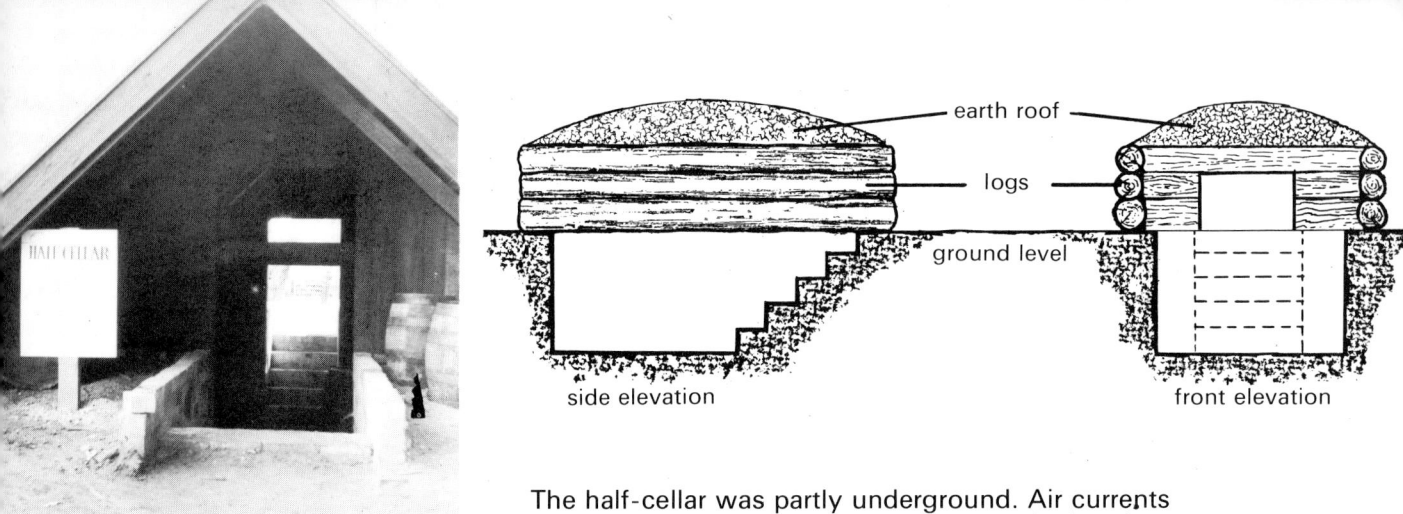

earth roof

logs

ground level

side elevation

front elevation

The half-cellar was partly underground. Air currents passed through the open ends, cooling the interior

The Half-cellar

Many outback homes had an outside store known as the *half-cellar* because it was partly underground. A pit was dug several feet deep, with a flight of steps leading down from ground level, and the whole excavation was then roofed over, either with wide-sloping eaves covered with a good layer of thatch or with log walls surmounted by an earth roof. An essential feature of the half-cellar was that it was open at both ends to allow cooling draughts to flow through the interior.

This principle was used in the draught cupboard situated in the centre of the house away from the heat of the stove. Holes bored in the floor allowed cool air from underneath the house to pass through the cupboard, keeping foodstuffs cooler than in an ordinary pantry.

A current of air was the cooling agent in another system for keeping food in hot weather—the draught cupboard which was constructed in the middle of the house. (Right) Evaporation kept the contents of this butter cooler fresh

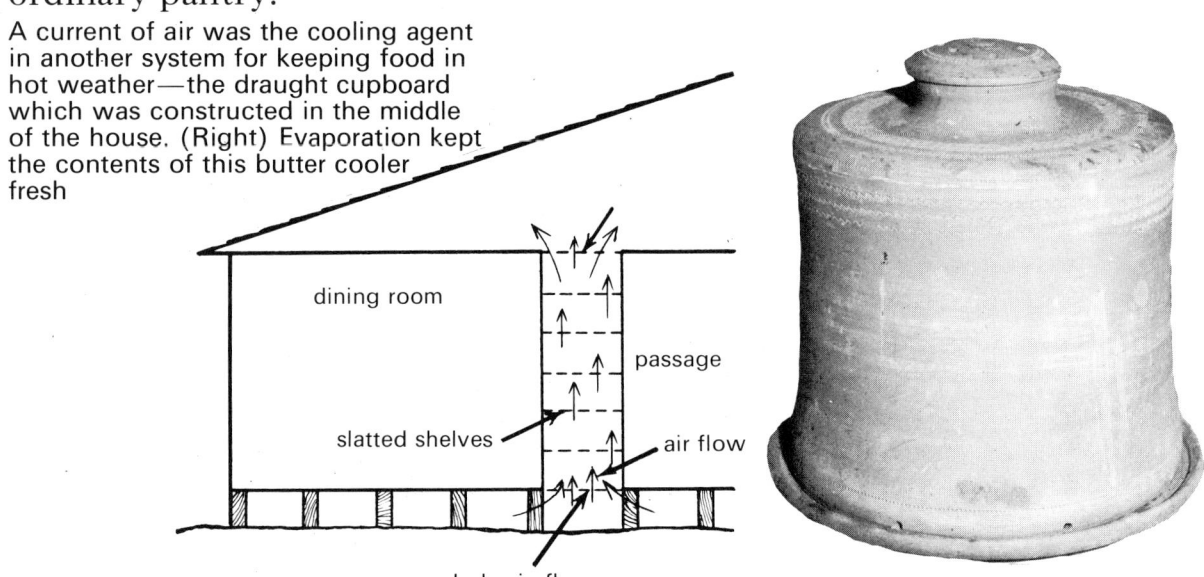

dining room

passage

slatted shelves

air flow

holes in floor

Store Room over a Tank

Many of the larger town houses had a cellar to serve as the cool room; if there was no cellar it was sometimes possible to make use of the household's water tanks. When Mrs Massary went to live in Melbourne in the 1850s she found herself contending with the heat, the flies and the high cost of water and milk. To begin with she kept three goats to supply milk for the family, and then she had a large brick store room built above the tank in the yard:

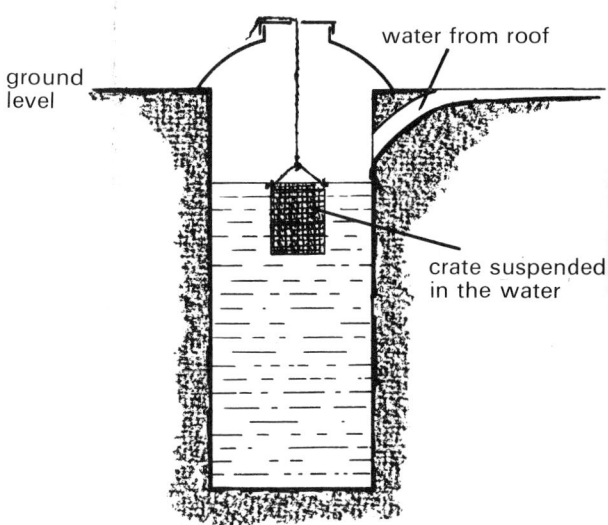

Another popular method was to hang perishable foods in a crate down the well

"The roof was of slate, very shelving and projecting; an opening was made through the roof and ceiling, so that a current of air might pass freely through the apartment; the windows were protected by fine *canvas wire* to prevent the flies coming in. We had shelves and cupboards made, also a trap door in the floor, so that the tank might be cleaned when required . . . The tank held fourteen or fifteen thousand gallons of water and, as our roof was slate, the water was perfectly good for every purpose and we never had to buy any, which was of some consequence to us, as it was sold for *4s (40 cents) a load or barrel.* The store room we found succeeded admirably; it was always deliciously cool and fresh." (Mrs I. Massary, *Social Life and Manners in Australia*, 1861.)

The term *well* has long been used in Australia to mean any form of underground water storage. In the country it meant a hole which was dug in order to reach supplies beneath the surface, and in settled areas it often meant a storage tank like Mrs Massary's which was filled with rainwater from the roof. In really hot weather housewives who had no other means of keeping food cool would fill a crate with bottles and jars and lower it into the well.

A useful device for keeping a pat of butter firm from one meal to the next was an evaporative cooler, a bell-shaped cover made of unglazed pottery. When this cover was placed over a dish containing water, the unglazed pottery absorbed the water and provided a cool surround for the butter in the centre of the dish.

A water bag. Note the mug hanging on a chain

Food Safes

In many homes drinking water was kept in a canvas bag hanging under the veranda where, thanks to the evaporation principle, it remained deliciously cool, even if it tasted slightly of the canvas! Meat too would hang in a sugar bag under the veranda or in the middle of a tree. Better still was the food *safe*, a well-constructed wooden box with scrubbed shelves and sides, and a hinged door of fine wire or zinc mesh which no fly could penetrate.

The Coolgardie Safe

There still remained the problem of keeping food cool in homes without a cellar or store room, and this could be met by buying a *Coolgardie Safe*. As you can see in the picture, this consisted of a tall stand with shelves and a small water tank on top from which wicks conveyed water by capillary action to a hessian curtain enclosing the entire stand. The sides of the wet curtain were supported and held clear of the frame by wires, and its hem rested in a tray from which the water could be drained and re-circulated. A more elaborate Coolgardie safe had limestone slab sides and whole store rooms were built on the same principle of conveying water down the sides of a container in order to keep the contents cool.

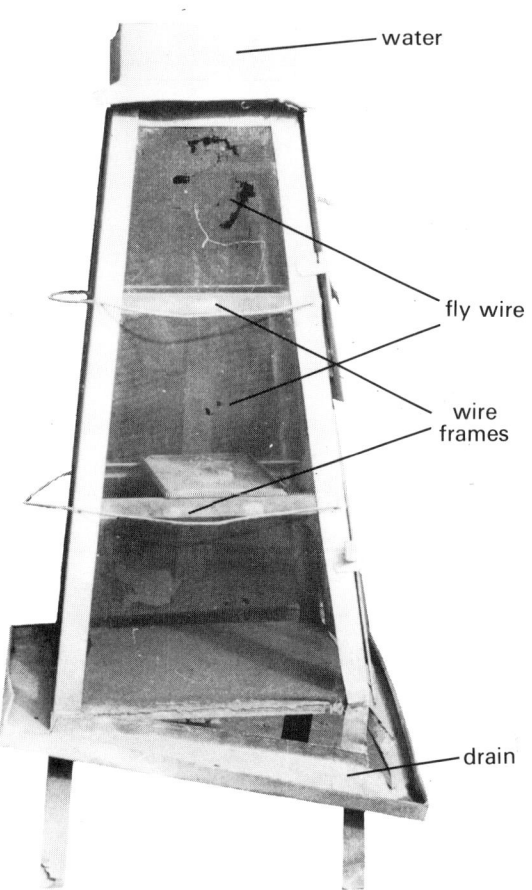

water

fly wire

wire frames

drain

A Coolgardie safe. Wicks ran from the water reservoir at the top, carrying water to the hessian curtain suspended from hooks round the top

Preserving Food

Even at the time when the First Fleet sailed to Australia, quite a lot was known about keeping food fit to eat; methods included salting, pickling, drying, adding sugar and keeping cold with ice. Sailors on long voyages lived mostly on hard dry biscuits and on meat which had been packed in layers of salt or pickled in brine; hence, in the early days of the colony when fresh meat was almost unobtainable, salt beef and pickled pork were the settlers' common fare.

It is amusing to find that, when Australia was producing more than enough meat for her own population, these same preserved meats, salt beef and pickled pork, were exported to England! This was in the 1860s when cattle plague caused a shortage of beef in Europe. Efforts were also made to market beef which had been dried on steam-heated iron plates, and in the 1870s the Victoria Meat Preserving Co. was exporting preserved beef which had been soaked in a chemical (calcium sulphate) and packed in casks filled with melted butter.

A country abbatoir, with windlasses for lifting the carcasses

Canning was introduced after a Frenchman had discovered how to preserve fruit in bottles. An English manufacturer tried packing meat in tin-coated iron containers, and from about 1812 the British Navy bought large quantities of canned meat, vegetables and soup for use by sailors at sea. The public was slow to take to this kind of food, especially after reports of meat going bad (this was due to the use of over-large cans in which the food in the centre was insufficiently heated). However, the scare died down and in 1847 a canning factory was started in Australia. Its goods were sold chiefly in the home market but by the 1860s large amounts of canned mutton were exported to England.

Cans containing meat and vegetables

Canned or "tinned" meat was rather coarse-grained and stringy, with lumps of yellow fat, but, although not very appetising, it was cheap and therefore a boon to the poor and to people living in remote districts.

Soldering on the lids of the cans in an early canning factory

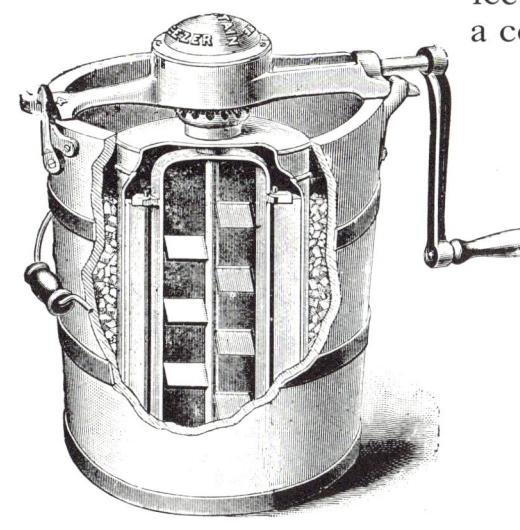

Ice cream freezers. Ice and salt were packed into the outer part of the bucket and the cream was poured into the central container where it was agitated, by means of paddles worked by the handle, to prevent ice crystals from forming

Ice Trade

Success in canning meat led to attempts to keep it in a frozen condition, but for a long time it was difficult to obtain sufficient quantities of ice. In 1839 the *Tartar* of Boston brought a cargo of ice from America, and this was used in *ice chests* which were too expensive for any but the richest citizens. The ice trade continued for some twenty years until ice-making machinery was set up in Sydney. A Scottish immigrant, named James Harrison, had made an ice-machine in 1850 and within a few years he was producing several tons of ice a day, first at Geelong and later in West Melbourne. At the Melbourne Exhibition of 1872 he exhibited an ice house which had kept meat in a perfect condition for months but, when used to take meat to England, the ice melted in the tropics and the scheme was a complete failure.

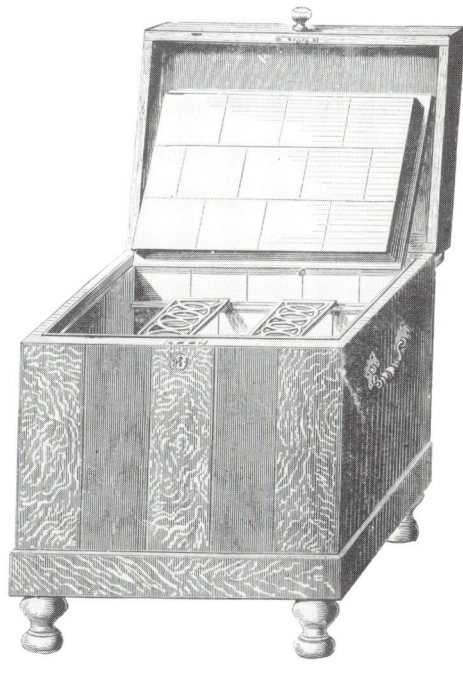

The first refrigerators so called were really ice chests and depended on a supply of ice from a dealer

Many ice chests were simple wooden structures. They needed frequent attention to avoid water leaking over the kitchen floor. One man drilled a hole in the floor

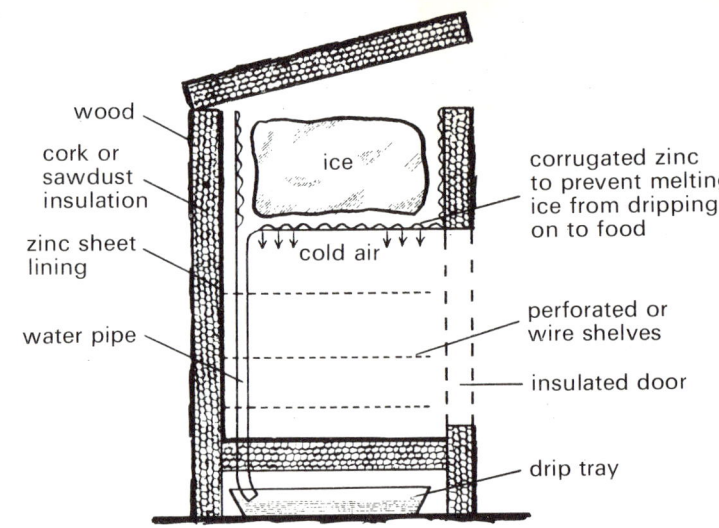

wood

cork or sawdust insulation

zinc sheet lining

water pipe

ice

cold air

corrugated zinc to prevent melting ice from dripping on to food

perforated or wire shelves

insulated door

drip tray

Refrigeration

Others carried on Harrison's work, using chambers cooled not with ice but by cold brine in pipes, and in 1880 the *Strathleven* carried forty tons of frozen beef and mutton from Australia to London. The meat, which had been sold fresh for $1\frac{1}{2}$d to 2d a pound (1–2 cents) in Melbourne, fetched $5\frac{1}{2}$d (5 cents) in London and refrigeration was now a proved success. Meat and many other foodstuffs could be carried from one side of the world to the other in refrigerated ships and kept for long periods in special warehouses and cold stores, but it was many years before the small domestic refrigerator came on to the market. In the meantime, until about 1950, most people used canned goods and kept food cool in the cellar, in the store room, in an ice chest, a Coolgardie safe or simply in a bag under the veranda.

One of the first Australian-made refrigerators, dating from 1934.

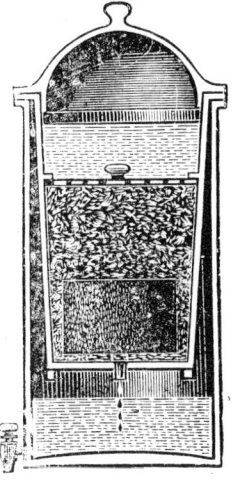

A rapid water filter containing a moulded carbon block and loose charcoal

A large container with a dome-shaped limestone filter

Water

As we have seen, water was a perpetual problem for the early settlers. Before the days of galvanised-iron roofs and iron tanks, they depended upon creeks, water holes, wells and storage tanks and, in time of low rainfall and drought, the water was far from pure. In *Days of Yore* Mary McMaugh remembered water being carted from the Torrens River and sold by the cask:

"the water being carted was execrable, what with tadpoles and other living creatures; the longer it rested the worse it became, and it was expensive as well."

Since it was highly dangerous to drink water like this, most homesteads had some sort of filter. The settlers would pour water through a mixture of charcoal and lime, or they used a limestone filter of the type manufactured by W. M. White of Melbourne. A dome-shaped dripstone filter was fitted inside an iron or pottery container and, after the water had passed through the limestone, it could be drawn off by a tap. Carbon was used in another type of purifier and from the 1880s a traveller could equip himself with a box of filter papers to use in his *Portable Filter for Tourists*.

The interior of a filter

A dripstone filter

A filter incorporated into the water supply (Jeffery's Patent Town and Country Filter). Mains pressure forced the water through the filter, along the pipe and into the tank where it was stored until it was needed

water tank

mains pressure

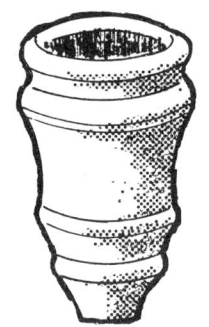

This small filter could be fastened to a water tap

According to the *Pictorial Australian* of June, 1893, a simple way to test suspected water was to "fill a clean pint bottle nearly full and to dissolve into it half a teaspoonful of loaf or granulated sugar. Cork the bottle and keep it warm for two days. If the water becomes cloudy or milky within forty-eight hours, it is unfit for domestic use."

People had so little faith in town water supplies that they would buy a patent filter to fix to the mains pipe so that all the household water passed through the filter and into a storage tank. Jeffrey's *Patent Town and Country Filter* was "specially recommended by Dr Gresswell, Chairman of the Board of Health", and an advertisement of 1900 informed readers that "Pure Water Means Good Health—Use the Eureka Water Filter and avoid all danger from Germs, Worms, and Animalculae of all kinds. The Eureka Water Filter fits any tap and can be removed in a moment."

In homes which possessed an underground storage tank water was raised by the bucketful or, better, by means of a pump in the yard. In well-to-do households a pressure pump might be fitted which delivered water under sufficient pressure to fill an overhead tank from which supplies could be piped round the house.

This kind of pump was used all over Australia to raise water from wells and underground tanks

Indoor sanitation was provided by chamber pots, which usually formed part of a richly patterned washstand set, or by a commode (below)

A typical toilet with a deep pit latrine

Sewage Disposal

It is a curious fact that in most countries a sewage disposal system is one of the last services to be provided. Australia was no different from the rest and for many years every householder had to make his own arrangements. The house might be well built and comfortably furnished but the privy or toilet, as we call it nowadays, was a ramshackle hut in the back yard. Sewage often flowed into open street drains and from time to time people died from cholera and typhoid through drinking polluted water.

As towns grew larger, better-off citizens had a cess pit dug in the garden, or they installed an earth closet like this 1860 one:

"Earth Closets (Rev. H. Moule's Patent) Manufactured and Sold Only by the Patent Earth Closet Company (Limited): These Earth Closets alone apply the dry earth system on a correct principle, as tested by a very large experience in their use in India and the United Kingdom. Upwards of 300 now in use in Melbourne and suburbs with perfect success. Price £4 and upwards; self-acting or pull. The supply of earth and cleansing contracted for by the company at a trifling annual charge."

This toilet was mounted on skids so that it could easily be shifted

Cess pits and earth closets had to be emptied at regular intervals, an operation which took place at night and was common in all large towns until the 1890s.

Under the old *single pan system* each householder provided a container that was carried to a cart and returned unwashed to the toilet. The *double pan service*, introduced in the 1890s and still in existence in some places, was more hygienic because a washed and sterilised pan was left in place of the used pan which was taken away to a depot, emptied and thoroughly cleansed.

An old mill at Parramatta—it made use of both wind and water power

A mill stone of the kind used in both windmills and water mills

A hand-turned mill was used in many homes to grind wheat into meal (this would produce brown wholemeal bread)

Mills

The windmills on Sydney's skyline which greeted early arrivals to Australia were built for flour milling. Every district had its mill driven either by water or by the wind, and Tasmania alone had over two hundred water-driven mills and ten windmills. Today there are very few remains of these once essential machines, though a fine one has been preserved in the centre of Perth.

In country homes corn had to be ground into flour by means of a steel hand mill. This was tedious work, and in his *A Homestead History* (written 1843–64, published 1942 by Melbourne University Press) Joyce describes how he built a windmill with sails nine feet across to turn a spindle on the hand mill which he fastened to a post in the open. Next he constructed a water mill so successfully that it ground his season's grain for several years. As a precaution against damage by floods he took the mill to pieces every year!

In many places the local mill was worked by a small steam engine which, like the water mill and the windmill, turned a pair of burr stones or, after 1885, the steel rollers of what was called Hungarian Roller Machinery.

Butter

One of the country housewife's more pleasant tasks was making butter. First she made sure that her hands and all utensils were scrupulously clean and then, in days before cream separators came into common use (they were introduced in the 1890s), she put the milk to *set* in shallow pans round the walls of the dairy. After forty-eight hours or so, the cream could be skimmed off and poured into the churn whose handle was turned in a steady, regular manner for some forty minutes. This caused the fat globules to come together and separate from the liquid buttermilk. When the butter had formed it could be salted, usually by washing it with brine, and patted into shape with wooden butter pats.

Various types of churn were used, from old-fashioned barrel churns, splash churns and upright plunge churns to more elaborate patent churns. They all produced butter by agitating cream until the fat was separated from the watery liquid. For home use the housewife would probably make her butter into round pats but, if it was to be sold, she used a mould to press it into one-pound blocks and stamped it with the farm's own butter stamp.

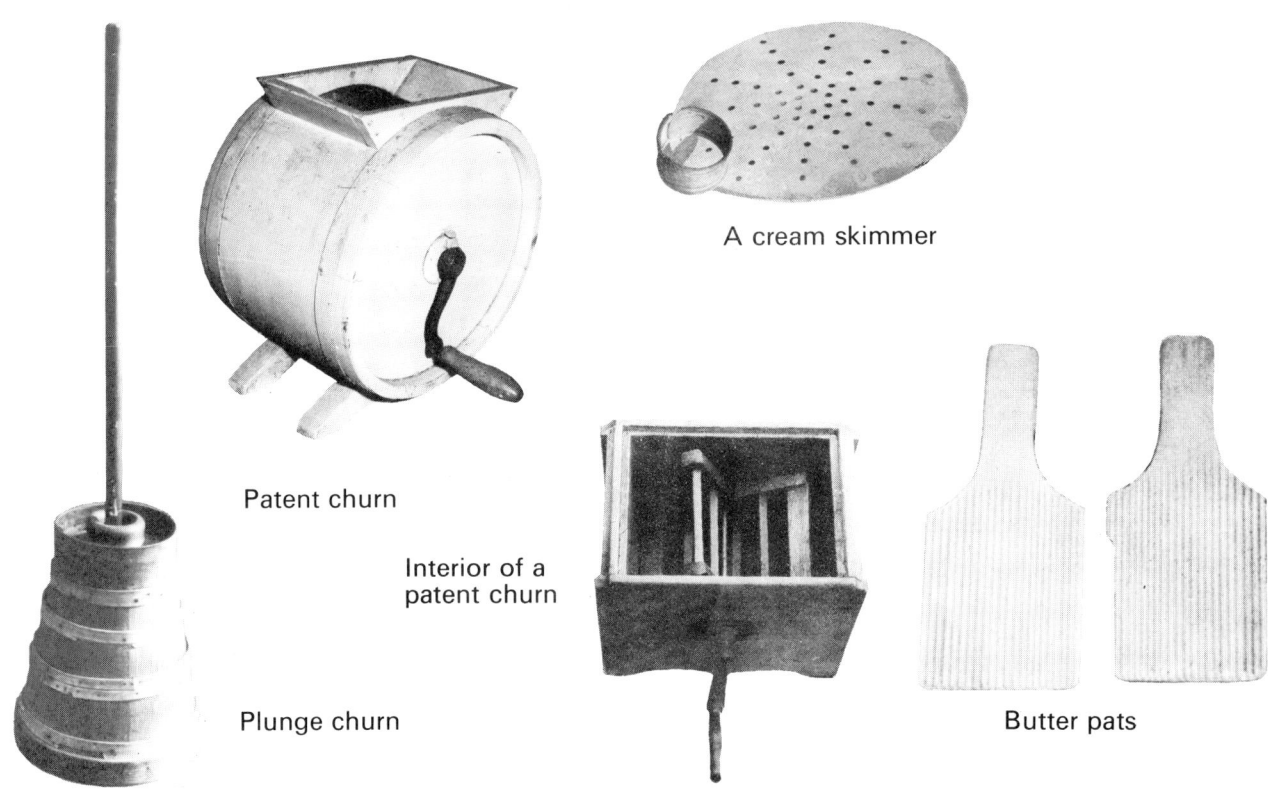

A cream skimmer

Patent churn

Interior of a patent churn

Plunge churn

Butter pats

Stoves

As we said earlier, the camp oven was the universal cooker of pioneer Australia.

Then, from about 1855, there appeared on the market the American Stove, an iron cooker which had most of the advantages of a fixed range—oven and hot plates—yet was transportable and therefore immensely useful to settlers going out to their distant selections, and building homes which might well prove to be temporary. The American Stove needed no brickwork or fixing; you merely set it down on its three sturdy legs, collected some wood and lit a fire.

The popularity of American Stoves caused Australian manufacturers to turn their attention to producing cooking ranges, ovens and "enclosed kitchens". At the Intercolonial Exhibition of 1866–67 the judges reported "a large and varied exhibit of these articles, for which there exists an immense demand, one firm alone making 2 000 per annum . . . a *Colonial Oven* measuring 24 inches by 12 inches by 18 inches can be supplied for 20 shillings ($2)."

A small American stove, easy to transport and use on a journey

Large American stoves provided hot plates for heating saucepans, an open fire for roasting, as well as an oven for baking

The double-walled Colonial Oven was bricked into a fireplace. When a fire was lit underneath, the heat and smoke passed between the double walls of the oven before escaping through the chimney

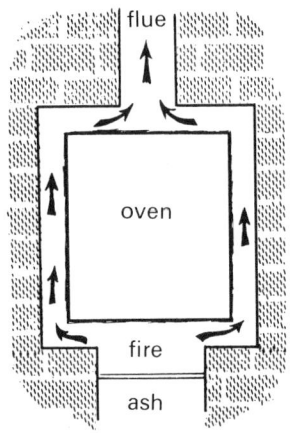

A Colonial Oven or two-fire stove. One fire would be lit underneath and another on top of the oven to heat it for baking. Saucepans and kettles could be placed on iron bars over the top fire

This type of Colonial Oven was simply an iron box with shelves and a hinged door; the double-walled Colonial Oven was bricked into a chimney and heated by the fire underneath and up both sides. A popular model was the *two-fire stove* in which the housewife lit fires above and below the oven. There were two- and three-oven ranges and for big households a "double-fire range, fourteen feet long, with five large ovens and two high pressure boilers for steam and water. Price £90 ($180)."

The *Pictorial Australian* of 1893 informed readers that Messrs A. Simpson & Son of Gawler Place, South Australia, were the first to manufacture ovens of any kind in Australia: "This was many years ago. The original Simpson's oven, protected by patent, is still the most widely used in the colony, over 15 000 are in use."

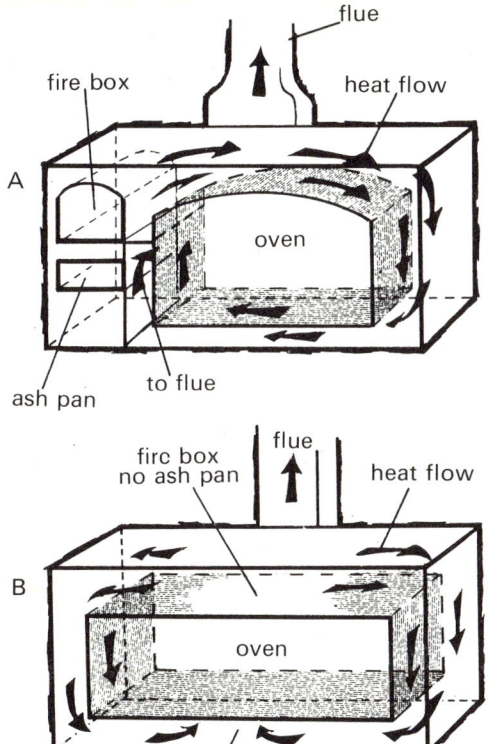

Metters Bros Improved Ovens

A Metters Bros Improved Oven with a fire over the oven. Note the tap at the left which provides hot water from a boiler at the side of the oven and fire box

Metters Bros' Improved Ovens came in three sizes, No. 1, at £3.10s ($7), burning 18-inch wood; No. 2, £4.10s ($9), burning 24-inch wood; and No. 3, £5.10s ($11), burning 30-inch wood. They were advertised in 1890 as requiring no brickwork and only one fire to "Roast, Bake and Boil. Can be used outside as well as inside the house." As you can see in the diagram the fire could be at the side—Type A—or on top of the oven—Type B, which seems to be a development of Simpson's Patent Oven and the double-walled Colonial Oven.

The Iron Fireplace, as made by T. McAlpine & Co. in 1900, was an iron box complete with chimney that had merely to be put in position wherever it was wanted. These fireplaces were therefore much used in schools, railway stations and selectors' homes in the bush where there were no supplies of brick or building stone.

An iron fireplace attached to a wooden building

A somewhat terrifying contraption introduced into Melbourne from America in 1890 was the *Quick Meal Gasolene Cooking Stove*. Described as "the wonder of the age", it was "not unlike a sewing machine in shape with the exception that there is an elevated reservoir from whence the oil is drawn which is used in the generating of gas." Apparently a gas generator converted the oil into gas which supplied from one to eight burners to suit the requirements of "the lonely bushman or the large hotel or coffee palace. The jets of the gas give splendid heat. Of danger there is none"!

Coal gas was produced in Australia at an early date; Sydney had gas street lighting in 1841, and the other capitals followed in the 1850s, but it was some time before gas was introduced into houses. This gas stove of about 1880 was made almost exactly like a wood fire stove with gas burners. The housewife needed these plates in a fire stove since they gave her some control over the heat (she could, for example, remove a plate in order to boil a kettle quickly and replace it for a saucepan whose contents had merely to simmer), but she could surely have controlled the heat of the gas stove by turning the jets up or down.

An early gas stove which closely resembles a wood-burning stove

An early twentieth-century gas stove. It still echoes the design of the American stove

Lighting

In the 18th century and during the first half of the 19th, the normal way of lighting a room was by candles. These were expensive and the settler often made do with a little lamp consisting of a bowl of fat, saved from the cooking pot, in which floated a piece of string. When the string or wick was lit, it produced a dim, smelly light. A slightly more elaborate lamp was the Scottish *cruzie*, known in Australia as a *slush lamp*. Molten fat was placed in the top bowl, the fat travelled by capillary action from one bowl to the other, supplying the string with sufficient fuel to produce a reasonable light.

Every wealthy home had its brass, silver and pewter candlesticks to light people to their rooms at night; fine branched candelabra stood in the centre of the dining table, and in the parlour people read novels and played the piano in the soft light of shaded candles. The best quality candles were made from beeswax or from blubber of the sperm whale and had cotton wicks to give a clear smokeless flame.

A slush lamp which used string soaked with cooking fat to produce a cheap, though smelly form of lighting

A candle lantern used to illuminate a room—it is designed so that the heat from the candle is deflected downwards, away from the inflammable calico ceiling. (Note the ham and the string of garlic hanging in the corner.)

A cotton wick would be placed in each section of this candle mould, and then melted tallow would be poured in and allowed to set

Kerosene lighting ranged from the lantern used out of doors to the elaborate lamps of the home

Brushes for cleaning the chimneys of oil lamps and an oil can for filling them

When Sarah Midgley wrote in her diary, "been busy making candles today", she had undoubtedly been helping her mother with yet another of the household tasks. Fat saved in the kitchen would have been melted and poured into *candle moulds* like the one in the picture, with a wick of string or perhaps simply a peeled rush in the centre. To make forty-eight dozen of these yellowish-brown candles, as the Midgleys did, must have taken a considerable time, but by the following day the fat had set and the finished candles were put away in the store room.

Oil or kerosene lamps, which came in the 1850s, were safer and more efficient than candles, and they supplied lighting for every kind of home until the turn of the century when gas lighting was introduced into town houses. The invention of the incandescent mantle turned the naked gas flame into a steady light which shone from a glass globe at the end of a gas pipe. Until the inter-war years, when electricity began to take over, gas remained the commonest form of lighting in town and cities.

Hot Water

Today most of us merely turn a tap to obtain hot or cold water, but until comparatively recent times piped water of any kind was regarded as a luxury. When water mains were first laid in towns, the pipes seldom ran into individual houses; at certain times of the day people collected water at stand-pipes in the main street. They paid a fee for each bucket or cask, though, if they could afford to do so, they could pay the water-carrier who called at the door.

When every drop of hot water had to be specially heated, housewives longed to possess one of the five-gallon *fountains* which stood permanently on top of the stove and had a tap from which hot water could be drawn. It was important, however, to remember to refill the fountain with cold!

A fountain

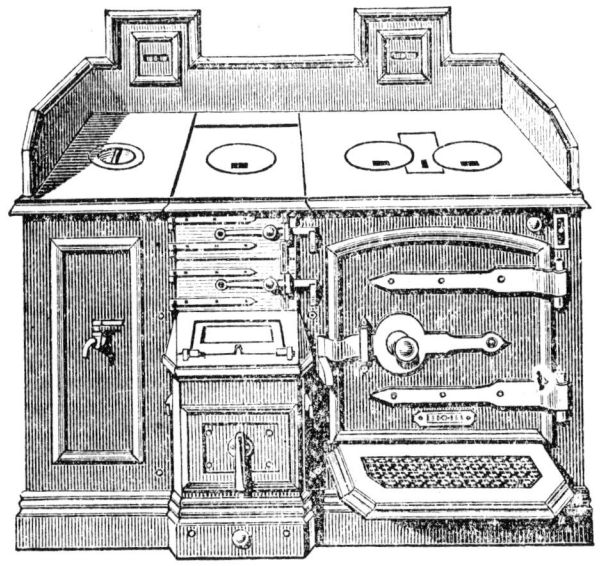

When elaborate kitchen ranges became popular, a fountain or water boiler was often incorporated at the side of the fire box. Later the boiler might be linked by pipes to the water supply and to baths and sinks to provide hot water on tap

The *Kitchener Three Oven Range with Grill*, commended by the judges of the 1866 Intercolonial Exhibition, must have been a splendid addition to the home, for it included "wrought iron boilers to supply water to the kitchen, scullery and bathroom." Mention of a bathroom makes it clear that this particular range was intended for large houses. Most people were lucky if they owned a plain washstand with jug and basin, though there was an aristocratic model, like the one in La Trobe's Cottage, whose basin was fitted with a plug and a short pipe to drain water into a receptacle below. A hip bath, like the one in the picture, was to be found in almost every home during Victoria's reign and until well into the present century. Anyone who has ever used a hip bath knows that it was the most inconvenient article ever invented, since it was impossible to sit, stand or lie comfortably in it. It was usually carried up to the bedroom or placed in front of the kitchen fire, so perhaps it was designed to encourage speedy bathing!

Two washstands, one from La Trobe's Cottage and the other of a humbler nature. Note the shaving mugs, one in silver and the other in pottery

A hip bath. There were also portable baths in which it was possible to lie down with some degree of comfort

Zinc baths were cheaper and lighter than a hip bath and they too had to be filled with buckets of water from the copper. Farmers often built an outhouse containing the copper, zinc bath and washing troughs, and this arrangement gave the bather greater privacy, though it was mighty cold hurrying back to the house on a winter's night.

Once bathing became popular, ways were found to supply hot water direct to the bath. Since *Jean's Patent Water Heater* had to be stoked with wood, coke or coal "brown or black", it may have been necessary to keep a supply of fuel in the bathroom! When gas was laid on to houses, a gas-fired bath heater might be fitted alongside the bath to produce a trickle of hot water from a tall cylinder similar to Jean's Heater.

In country districts the *chip heater* was very popular and one of the authors of this book remembers the rejoicing when a chip bath heater was installed in his home. Until then hot water had been carried in from the copper, but *Malley's Heater* proved to be much more efficient and convenient; a newspaper and a handful of chips —bark, small twigs, etc.—quickly provided enough hot water for a bath.

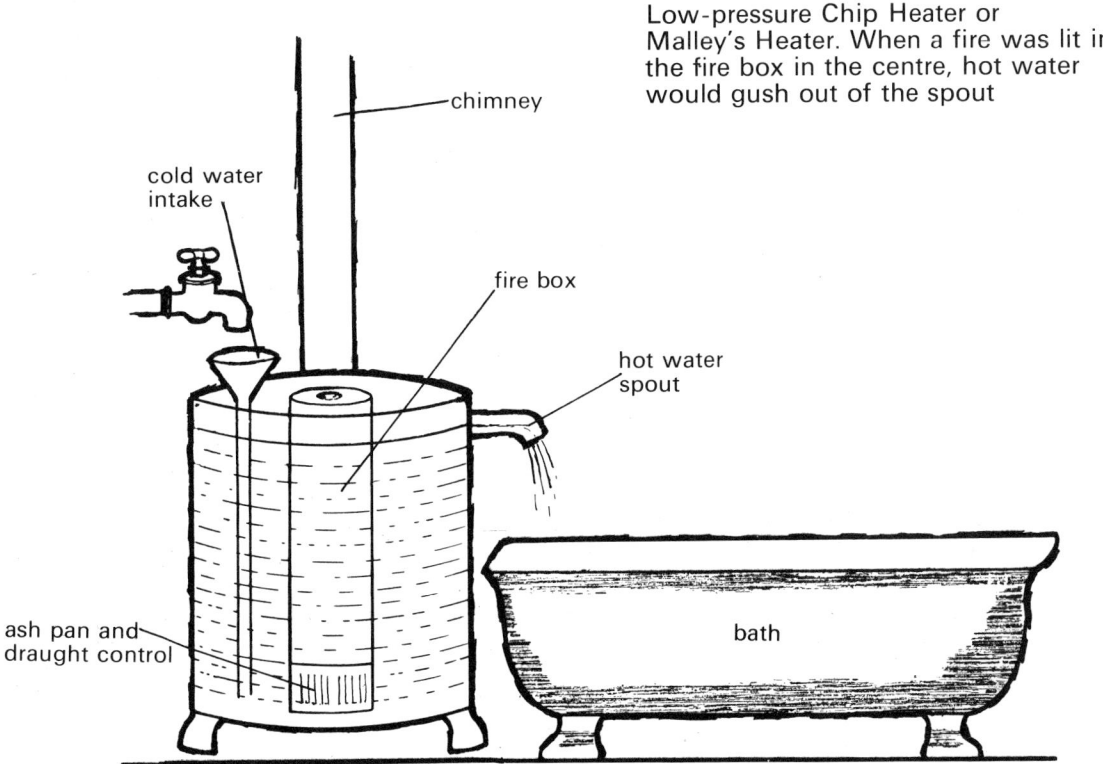

Low-pressure Chip Heater or Malley's Heater. When a fire was lit in the fire box in the centre, hot water would gush out of the spout

chimney

cold water intake

fire box

hot water spout

ash pan and draught control

bath

Some of the handles the housewife turned in her daily work: (from top to bottom) sewing machine, washing machine, egg beater

Turning Handles

Ever since the first settlements were made in Australia, there has been a constant flow of changes and improvements in the home, and these improvements have almost always had one object—to take the hard toil out of housekeeping. For generations the housewife hardly ever stopped turning handles and lifting heavy weights.

She needed to turn a handle to work her washing machine, mangle, wringer, butter churn, mincer, sewing machine, knife machine, steel mill.

She had to lift coal, wood and numberless buckets of water; she had to work the pump handle, scrub floors, sweep, polish and black-lead grates by hand. She needed strong arms and a strong back and we salute her!

Seventy Years Ago

To end this book and to sum up some of the changes which have taken place in one lifetime, here is part of a taped conversation with an elderly lady named Mrs Joyce:

"I was brought up on a farm near Melbourne. That would be about seventy years ago. It was a small farm and we used to kill our pig and make our own bacon. We cured the pig in a wooden tub. We had to rub it with sugar and saltpetre. All the intestines were turned inside out and put in a bucket of lime water that was changed every day for three days, and we had those with a beaten-up egg and fried. Some were used to make sausage skins and the skins for black puddings. There was nothing lost of that pig except the squeal—ears, tail and all were cooked and eaten. Kidneys and liver were eaten.

"Every morning the pig was lifted out of the big wooden tub and it was rubbed with its own sugar and stuff. It was then hung up on the rafter in the kitchen and, when I was very hungry, I'd take a big knife and stand on the table and cut a big lump off, cook it on the stove and then run up the paddock and eat it.

"We always had a one-fire stove. Grandma had a two-fire stove, the fire on the top and the fire underneath—that was the old Colonial Oven. She came out here in 1852. Lot of people then did not have stoves when I was a child; they only had the camp oven and they made bread and all in those. Mum used to bake the bread in a brick oven and supply everybody.

"We used to gather the milk thistles in the fields, wash them well, cut them up. We made dressing of cream and vinegar. Dandelions too—they were rather bitter but we made salad of them in the same way.

"In those days we never grew a tomato. Nobody ate many tomatoes then. People didn't eat the same things as they eat now. They ate a lot more potatoes. We only had potatoes in the winter and pumpkin and heaps of fruit.

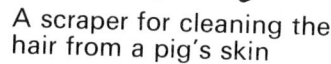

A scraper for cleaning the hair from a pig's skin

Dutch oven for grilling chops in front of the fire

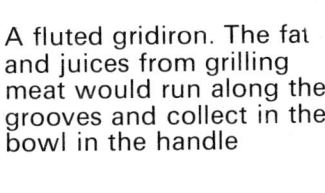

A fluted gridiron. The fat and juices from grilling meat would run along the grooves and collect in the bowl in the handle

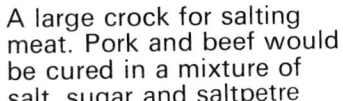

A large crock for salting meat. Pork and beef would be cured in a mixture of salt, sugar and saltpetre

A small churn such as Mrs Joyce's family might have used

A knife-cleaning machine. The knives were placed, blade downwards, in slots at the top; a little cleaning powder was poured in and the handle was turned to rotate brushes over the knife blades

A grooved rolling pin for crushing oats

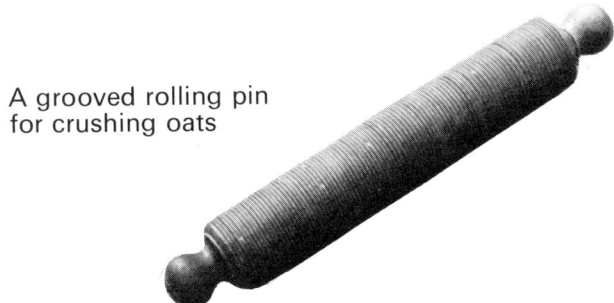

"We had plenty of good suet puddings with apples in and milk puddings and a lot of rice pudding. We always ate well; we had rabbits and milk and fowls and a pig.

"The old hens were allowed to run loose. I don't think we ever fed them and we'd have to go looking for the eggs. Sometimes we'd come home and they'd be all rotten. Sometimes they were full of chickens.

"Making butter? Well, you warmed the milk to a certain degree and there was that little log house, and round the wall there was these pannikins, and you let it stand twenty-four hours and skimmed it off with a little thing that had holes in it. You know, a little skimmer, and then you made the butter and that. Mrs Cant had a plunge churn. We had a little churn you turned around. In the very hot weather we'd put it down the well in a bucket to keep it cool.

"If you wanted to cool drink down, you hung it down the well on a string. We kept meat in a chaff bag with a board under the tree.

"We never had any tanks. We only had the well and pulled the water up in the bucket. It was terrible hard work doing the washing.

"We didn't have a wash-house in those early days. The copper was outside on a couple of bricks, and the big tub was underneath the pear tree, and we pulled the water up out of the well and we wrung the washing with our hands. It took all day.

"When I was little and we'd run out of water, Dad would put the copper and the tub and everything in the dray, and off they go to a dam and do the washing there, and hang it on the bushes to dry.

"Made our own soap? Yes. Kerosene tin of water, thirteen pounds of fat, a couple of pounds of caustic soda and some borax. That was all. Some people used wood ashes instead of caustic soda.

"We made our candles too. We had the candle moulds and the snuffer thing to trim the candles.

"We had a tub and we bathed in the bedroom in the summer and in the winter in front of a big open fire.

"No, we didn't use wooden yokes for carrying. Only the Chinese gardeners used them. Ah Yet used to grow vegetables and take them round in his basket to sell.

An early pressure cooker

A hot water bottle

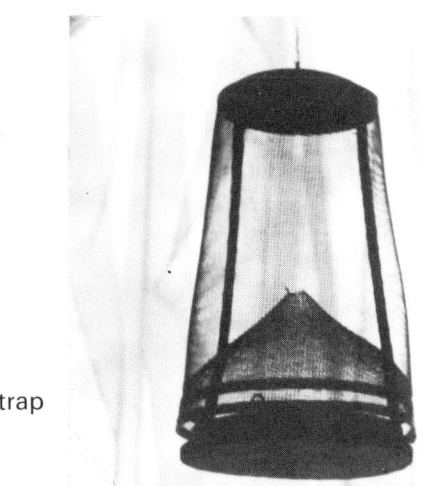

A fly trap

"There was an old Indian called Hokkam Ghan, and he used to come along and stay the night with his two horses and his wagon, and if we were killing a sheep, he would ask if he could kill it. He would say some of his little prayers over it and then he could eat some of it . . . We got mainly drapery from old Hokkam, pieces of material, not much made-up material. On the back of his cart he had a little platform where he carried his hay, and he also carried his chickens with their legs tied up, and he'd make his curry and damper down there on the flat.

"I went into service when I was a girl. The first sink I ever saw was when I went to town and worked for some Jews. I was fifteen then.

"No, you couldn't keep things cool, even in town. The milkman came round with the milk twice a day. If he didn't, it was sour by night. He came round with his can and his little pint measure, and flies by the thousand.

"When the butcher came round, the meat wasn't cut up much. You had to go out to the cart and he cut it up on the tailboard while we swished the flies.

"I've seen the whole roof of a bakehouse black with flies, and they threw something up and set them all on fire, and then swept them up by the dustpan full.

"Yes, things have changed a lot since those days . . ."

A sitting room of 1878

Places to Visit

When the authors were writing this book they could find no other books specially written about pioneer home life, but many of the things mentioned in this text can be found in folk museums and historic homes, many of which are open to the public. Below is a list of some of the places you may be able to visit to learn more about the daily life of the past.

Canberra
Horse Era Museum, Canberra*

New South Wales
Carisbrook, Lane Cove
Experiment Farm Cottage, Parramatta
Folk Museum, Cooma*
Hambledon Cottage, Parramatta
Jindera Museum, near Albury*
Old Government House, Parramatta
Vaucluse House, Vaucluse
Wentworth Museum, Wentworth
Wilberforce (authentic Australian settlers' village)

Queensland
Advance Town Cottage*
James Cook Historical Museum, Cooktown
Ormiston House, Cleveland
Pioneer Cottage, Buderim
Wolston House, Wacol, Brisbane

South Australia
Birdwood Mill Museum, Birdwood
Burra Museum, Burra
Dingley Dell, Port Macdonnell
The Grange, Adelaide
Kapunda Museum, Kapunda
Murray Bridge Museum
National Trust Museum, Gawler
Tanunda Museum, Tanunda

Tasmania
Clarendon House, near Evandale
Entally National House, Hadspen*
Franklin House, Franklin Village
The Grove, George Town
Narryna, Hobart
Runnymede, Newton
Van Diemen's Lane Memorial Folk Museum*

Victoria
Burke Museum, Beechworth*
Como House, Melbourne*
Henry Handel Richardson's Home, Chiltern*
Historical Museum, Eaglehawk*
Kelly Museum, Benalla*
Kyneton Museum*
La Trobe's Cottage, Melbourne*
Montrose Cottage, Ballarat*
Schwerkolt's Cottage, Nunawading*
Sovereign Hill, Ballarat
Swan Hill Folk Museum*
Wedderburn Museum, Wedderburn.

Western Australia
Coolgardia Ghost Town*
The Golden Mile Museum, Kalgoorlie
The Old Farm, Strawberry Hill, Albany
Old Mill, South Perth*
The Old Newcastle Gaol, Tooday

* Exhibits from this house or museum are included in the photographs in the book or reference is made in the text.

Index